Nothing But
Beginner Vocab
Spanish Edition

By

John Robert Loehr

Copyright 2023
by John R. Loehr
All rights reserved

ISBN: **979-8-9872118-3-0**

Printed in the United States of America

First Edition

Contents

Introduction

This is my second Spanish vocabulary book, though, retrospectively, it should have been my first. This book is tailored to the needs of the new to intermediate student of Spanish, while my other book is far more comprehensive and advanced. This book will introduce students to vocabulary ranging from levels A1 to B2. This is not a vocabulary book for an advanced or even an advanced intermediate student. It is best suited to meet the goals of the newbie to the intermediate Spanish student. This book contains no grammar at all. It was written to study and learn new Spanish words and nothing more. Simply put, it is *Nothing but Beginner Vocabulary*.

The way in which *Nothing but Beginner Vocab: Spanish Edition* is arranged will make learning Spanish easier. It is organized around the Common European Framework of Reference for Languages (CEFR), which is an international standard for describing language ability on a six point scale from A1 for beginners, up to C2 for those who have mastered a language (Common European Framework of Reference 2022).

Each chapter covers a CEFR level, beginning with A1 and ending with B2. Each chapter is further sub-divided according to whether it is a noun, verb, adjective, adverb, or special word. At the end of each sub-chapter (A1 Nouns, for example), you will be quizzed to test your new knowledge and retention. At the end of each chapter (Level A2, for example), there will be a section test which is more comprehensive. To conclude the book, there is an enormous final exam covering everything you will have learned. Take the tests seriously. Do not advance until you get at least a 90% on a language level final exam. If you can get a 90% on the comprehensive final exam, you will possess the vocabulary necessary for basic fluency. By that I mean to say you will possess the vocabulary necessary to be able to understand and hold basic conversations in Spanish. You won't have the grammar, but if you focus on the vocabulary, the rest will come in time with experience and practice. It is imperative that you practice what you learn.

May the words come easily to you! I hope you enjoy your language learning journey!

Level A1 Vocabulary

Level A1 is the first level of Spanish in the Common European Framework of Reference (CEFR). This level is considered a true "beginner". An A1 level of Spanish would be sufficient for only very simple interactions. According to the official CEFR guidelines, someone at the A1 level in Spanish:

- Can understand and use familiar everyday expressions and very basic phrases aimed at the satisfaction of needs of a concrete type (Council of Europe 2022).
- Can introduce him/herself and others and can ask and answer questions about personal details such as where he/she lives, people he/she knows and things he/she has (Council of Europe 2022).
- Can interact in a simple way provided the other person talks slowly and clearly and is prepared to help (Council of Europe 2022).

A1 Nouns

English Word	Spanish Translation
action	acción
activity	actividad
actor	actor
actress	actriz
address	dirección
adult	adulto
advice	consejo
afternoon	tarde
age	años/edad
air	aire
airport	aeropuerto
animal	animal
answer	respuesta
apartment	departamento
apple	manzana
April	abril
area	área/zona
arm	brazo
art	arte
article	artículo
artist	artista
August	agosto
aunt	tía
baby	bebé
back	espalda/resplado
bag	bolso
ball	bola/balón/pelota
banana	plátano
band	banda

bank (money)	banco (dinero)
bar	bar/barra
baseball	béisbol
basketball	baloncesto
bat	bate/murciélago
bath	bañera
bathroom	baño
beach	playa
bed	cama
bedroom	dormitorio/recamara
beer	cerveza
beginning	comienzo
bicycle	bicicleta
bike	bici
bill	factura/recibo
bird	pájaro
birthday	cumpleaños
black	negro
blog	blog
blue	azul
boat	barco
body	cuerpo
book	libro
boot	bota
bottle	botella
box	caja
boy	niño
boyfriend	novio
bread	pan
break	descanso/receso
breakfast	desayuno
brother	hermano
brown	marrón

building	edificio
bus	autobús
business	negocio
butter	manteca/mantequilla
cafe	cafetería
cake	pastel
call	llamada
camera	cámara
capital	capital
car	coche
card	tarjeta
career	carrera
carrot	zanahoria
cat	gato
CD	CD
cent	centavo
center	centro
chair	silla
change	cambio
chart	gráfico
cheese	queso
chicken	pollo
child	niño
children	niños
chocolate	chocolate
city	ciudad
class	clase
classroom	salón de clases/aula
clock	reloj
clothes	ropa
club	club
coat	saco/abrigo
coffee	café
cold	frío

college	colega/colegio universitario
color	color
company	empresa/compañia
computer	computadora
concert	concierto
conversation	conversación
cooking	cocinando
cost	costo
country	país
course	curso
cousin	primo
cow	vaca
cream	crema
culture	cultura
cup	taza
customer	cliente
dad	papá
dance	danza
dancer	bailarín
dancing	bailando
date	fecha
daughter	hija
day	día
December	diciembre
description	descripción
design	diseño
desk	escritorio
detail	detalle
dialogue	diálogo
dictionary	diccionario
diet	dieta
difference	diferencia
dinner	cena

dish	plato/platillo
doctor	doctor/médico
dog	perro
dollar	dólar
door	puerta
dress	vestido
drink	bebida
driver	conductor
ear	oído
east	este
egg	huevo
elephant	elefante
email	email
end	final/fin
euro	euro
evening	anochecer/tarde
event	evento
exam	exámen
example	ejemplo
exercise	ejercicio
eye	ojo
face	cara/rostro
fact	hecho
fall	otoño
family	familia
farm	granja
farmer	granjero
father	padre
favorite	favorito
February	febrero
feeling	sentimiento
feet	pies
festival	festival
fine	multa

fire	fuego
fish	pescado
flight	vuelo
floor	piso
flower	flor
food	comida/alimento
foot	pie
football	fútbol
form	formulario/forma
Friday	viernes
friend	amigo
front	frente
fruit	fruta
fun	divertida
future	futuro
game	juego
garden	jardín
geography	geografía
girl	chica/niña
girlfriend	novia
glass	vaso/vidrio
grandfather	abuelo
grandmother	abuela
grandparent	abuelo
gray	gris
group	grupo
guess	adivinanza
guitar	guitarra
gym	gimnasia
hair	pelo
half	medio
hand	mano
hat	sombrero

head	cabeza
health	salud
hello	hola
help	ayuda
history	historia
hobby	pasatiempo
home	casa/hogar
homework	tarea
horse	caballo
hospital	hospital
hotel	hotel
hour	hora
house	casa
husband	marido/esposo
ice	hielo
ice cream	helado
idea	ocurrencia/idea
information	información
interest	interés
internet	Internet
interview	entrevista
island	isla
jacket	chaqueta/saco
January	enero
jeans	vaqueros/pantalon de mezclilla
job	trabajo
juice	jugo
July	julio
June	junio
key	llave/clave
kind (type)	tipo
kitchen	cocina
land	tierra/terreno
language	idioma

Level A1 Vocabulary

laugh	risa
left	izquierda
leg	pierna
lesson	lección
letter	carta
library	biblioteca
life	vida
light	luz
line	línea
lion	león
list	lista
love	amor
lunch	comida
machine	máquina
magazine	revista
mall	centro comercial
man	hombre
map	mapa
March	marzo
market	mercado
match	fósforo
May	mayo
meal	comida
meaning	sentido/significado
meat	carne
meeting	cita/reunión/encuentro
member	miembro
men	hombres
menu	menú
message	mensaje
meter	metro
midnight	medianoche
mile	milla

milk	leche
minute	minuto
mistake	error
model	modelo
mom	mamá
moment	momento
Monday	lunes
money	dinero
month	mes
morning	mañana
mother	mamá
mountain	montaña
mouse	ratón
mouth	boca
movie	película
museum	museo
music	música
name	nombre
neighbor	vecino
neighborhood	vecindario/barrio
news	noticias
newspaper	periódico
night	noche
north	norte
nose	nariz
note	nota
November	noviembre
number	número
nurse	enfermera
object	objeto
ocean	océano
October	octubre
office	oficina
onion	cebolla

opinion	opinión
opposite	opuesto
orange	naranja
order	órden
outside	afuera
page	página
paint	pintura
painting	cuadra/pintura
pair	par
pants	pantalones
paper	papel
paragraph	párrafo
parent	padre
park	parque
part	parte
partner	compañero
party	fiesta
passport	pasaporte
past	pasado
pen	lapicero
pencil	lápiz
people	personas/gente
pepper	pimienta
period	período
person	persona
phone	teléfono
photo	foto
photograph	fotografía
phrase	frase
piano	piano
picture	fotografía/imágen
piece	trozo/pieza
pig	cerdo

pink	rosa
place	lugar/sitio
plain	llanura/plano
plane	avión
plant	planta
play	juego/obra
player	jugador
point	punto
police	policía
policeman	policía
pool	piscina/alberca
post	publicación
potato	papa
pound	libra
practice	práctica
present	presente
price	precio
problem	problema
product	producto
program	programa
project	proyecto
purple	púrpura/morado
quarter	cuarto
question	pregunta
radio	radio
rain	lluvia
reader	lector
reading	leyendo
reason	razón
red	rojo
report	informe
restaurant	restaurante
result	resultado
return	vuelta/retorno/regreso

Level A1 Vocabulary

rice	arroz
right	correcto/derecho/derecha
river	río
road	camino/carretera
room	habitación
routine	rutina
rule	regla
salad	ensalada
salt	sal
sandwich	emparedado/sándwich
Saturday	sábado
school	escuela
science	ciencia
scientist	científico
second (unit of time)	segundo
section	sección
sentence	frase
September	septiembre
sheep	oveja
shirt	camisa
shoe	zapato
shop	tienda
shopping	compras
show	show/espectáculo
shower	ducha
singer	cantante
sister	hermana
situation	situación
skill	habilidad
skirt	falda
snake	serpiente
snow	nieve
son	hijo

song	canción
sound	sonido
soup	sopa
south	sur
space	espacio
spelling	ortografía
sport	deporte
spring	primavera
star	estrella
statement	declaración
station	estación
stop	parada
store	tienda
story	historia
street	calle
student	estudiante/alumno
study	estudio
style	estilo
subject	sujeto/tema
success	éxito
sugar	azúcar
summer	verano
sun	sol
Sunday	domingo
supermarket	supermercado
sweater	suéter
swimming	nadando
table	mesa
taxi	taxi
tea	té
teacher	profesor/maestro
team	equipo
teenager	adolescente
telephone	teléfono

television	televisión
tennis	tenis
test	Prueba/ensayo
text	texto
thanks	gracias
theater	teatro
thing	cosa
Thursday	jueves
ticket	boleto/billete/entrada
time	hora/tiempo
title	título
today	hoy
toilet	inodoro
tomato	tomate
tomorrow	mañana
tonight	esta noche
tooth	diente
topic	tema
tourist	turista
town	ciudad/pueblo
traffic	tráfico
train	tren
travel	viajes/viaje
tree	árbol
trip	viaje
truck	camión
T-shirt	camiseta
Tuesday	martes
turn	turno
TV	televisión/televisor
type	tipo
umbrella	paraguas
uncle	tío

university	universidad
vacation	vacación
vegetable	vegetal
video	video
visit	visita
visitor	visitante
waiter	camarero/mesero/mozo
walk	paseo/caminata
wall	pared
watch	reloj
water	agua
way	forma/manera
weather	tiempo/clima
website	sitio web
Wednesday	miércoles
week	semana
weekend	fin de semana
west	oeste
white	blanco
wife	esposa
window	ventana
wine	vino
winter	invierno
woman	mujer
word	palabra
work	trabajo
worker	trabajador
world	mundo
writer	escritor
writing	escritura
yard	yarda/patio/patio trasero
year	año
yellow	amarillo
yesterday	ayer/el dia de ayer

A1 Nouns Quiz

1.	pollo	A.	rice
2.	tienda	B.	bill
3.	año	C.	drink
4.	fiesta	D.	house
5.	tío	E.	egg
6.	arroz	F.	classroom
7.	cocina	G.	year
8.	bebida	H.	place
9.	chica/muchacha	I.	question
10.	risa	J.	airport
11.	aeropuerto	K.	map
12.	factura	L.	week
13.	salón de clases	M.	information
14.	vuelo	N.	job
15.	casa	O.	chicken
16.	pregunta	P.	name
17.	cebolla	Q.	visit
18.	huevo	R.	kitchen
19.	lugar/sitio	S.	girl
20.	información	T.	onion
21.	visitar	U.	party
22.	mapa	V.	flight
23.	trabajo	W.	laughter
24.	nombre	X.	uncle
25.	semana	Y.	store

Answer Key

1. O
2. Y
3. G
4. U
5. X
6. A
7. R
8. C
9. S
10. W
11. J
12. B
13. F
14. V
15. D
16. I
17. T
18. E
19. H
20. M
21. Q
22. K
23. N
24. P
25. L

A1 Verbs

English Word	Spanish Translation
add	agregar/añadir
agree	acordar/aceptar
am	soy
answer	responder
are	estan/son
arrive	llegar
ask	preguntar
be	ser/estar
become	convertir
been	estado
began	comenzó
begin	empezar/comenzar
believe	creer
born	nacer
bought	comprado
break	romper/quebrar
bring	traer
build	construir
buy	comprar
call	llamar
came	vino/llegó
can	poder
cannot	no poder
carry	llevar
caught	capturado/atrapado
check	verificar/comprobar
choose	escoger/eligir
clean	limpiar

climb	escalar
close	cerrar
come	venir
compare	comparar
complete	completar
cook	cocinar
correct	corregir
cost	costar
could	pudo/podria
create	crear
cut	cortar
dance	bailar
decide	decidir
describe	describir
design	diseñar
die	morir
discuss	discutir
do	hacer
draw	dibujar
dress	vestir
drink	beber
drive	conducir
eat	comer
end	terminar
enjoy	disfrutar
exercise	ejercitar
explain	explicar
fall	caer
feel	sentir
fill	llenar
find	encontrar
finish	finalizar/terminar
fly	volar
follow	seguir

forget	olvidar
form	formar
get	conseguir
give	dar
go	ir
grow	crecer
guess	adivinar
happen	ocurrir/suceder
hate	odiar
have	tener
hear	oír/escuchar
help	ayudar
hope	esperar
imagine	imaginar
improve	mejorar
include	incluir
interview	entrevistar
introduce	introducir
is	es
join	unir
keep	guardar/mantaner
know	saber
laugh	reír
learn	aprender
leave	dejar/salir
let	dejar
like	gustar
list	listar
listen	escuchar
live	vivir
look	buscar/mirar
lose	perder
love	amar

make	fabricar/hacer
match (contest/correspond)	hacer coincidir
mean	significar
meet	reunirse
miss	extrañar
name	nombrar
need	necesitar
open	abrir
order	ordenar
paint	pintar
park	aparcar/estacionar
pay	pagar
plan	planificar
play	tocar/jugar
post	publicar
practice	practicar
prefer	preferir
prepare	preparar
put	poner
rain	llover
read	leer
relax	relajarse
remember	recordar
repeat	repetir
return	devolver
ride	montar
run	correr/ejecutar
say	decir
see	ver
sell	vender
send	enviar
share	compartir
shop	hacer compras
should	debería

Level A1 Vocabulary

show	mostrar
sing	cantar
sit	sentarse
sleep	dormir
snow	nevar
sound	sonar
speak	hablar
spell	deletrear
spend	gastar/pasar
stand	estar de pie
start	comenzar/empezar
stay	quedarse
stop	detener/dejar/parar
study	estudiar
swim	nadar
take	llevar/tomar
talk	hablar
teach	enseñar
tell	contar/decir
test	probar/comprobar/ensayar
thank	agradecer
think	pensar
travel	viajar
try	intentar/probar
turn	doblar/girar
understand	comprender
use	usar
visit	visitar
wait	esperar
wake	despertarse
walk	caminar
want	desear/querer
wash	lavar

watch	ver
wear	vestir
win	ganar
work	trabajar
would	haría
write	escribir
change	cambiar

A1 Verbs Quiz

1.	recordar	A.	sit
2.	esperar	B.	improve
3.	responder	C.	bring
4.	limpiar	D.	open
5.	sentarse	E.	prefer
6.	hablar	F.	drive
7.	mejorar	G.	wait
8.	encontrar	H.	have
9.	traer	I.	visit
10.	comprender	J.	go
11.	abierto	K.	understand
12.	aprender	L.	join
13.	hacer	M.	make
14.	preferir	N.	need
15.	conducir	O.	answer
16.	tener	P.	see
17.	visitar	Q.	give
18.	ir	R.	talk
19.	unirse	S.	put
20.	saber	T.	learn
21.	fabricar/hacer	U.	know
22.	necesidad	V.	remember
23.	poner	W.	do
24.	ver	X.	find
25.	dar	Y.	clean

Answer Key

1. V
2. G
3. O
4. Y
5. A
6. R
7. B
8. X
9. C
10. K
11. D
12. T
13. W
14. E
15. F
16. H
17. I
18. J
19. L
20. U
21. M
22. N
23. S
24. P
25. Q

A1 Adjectives

English Word	Spanish Translation
afraid	atemorizado
amazing	impresionante
angry	enojado
awesome	increíble
bad	mala
beautiful	hermosa
best	el mejor
better	mejor
big	grande
black	negro
blond	rubio
blue	azul
bored	aburrido
boring	aburrido
brown	marrón
busy	ocupado
capital	capital
cheap	barato
clean	limpio
cold	frío
common	común
complete	completo
cool	frío/fresco
correct	correcto
dangerous	peligroso
dark	oscuro
dear	querido/estimado
delicious	delicioso

different	diferente
difficult	difícil
dirty	sucio
early	temprano
east	este
easy	fácil
excited	emocionado
exciting	excitante/emocionante
expensive	costoso/caro
extra	extra
false	falso
family	familia
famous	famoso
fantastic	fantástico
fast	rápido
fat	gordo
favorite	favorito
final	final/último
free	gratis/libre
friendly	amistoso
front	frente
full	lleno/completo
funny	gracioso
good	bueno
gray	gris
great	estupendo/gran
green	verde
happy	feliz/contento
hard	duro
healthy	sano
high	elevado/alto
hot	caliente
hungry	hambriento
important	importante

interested	interesado
interesting	interesante
large	grande
late	tarde
left	izquierda
light	ligero
little	poco
local	local
long	largo
main	principal
married	casado
modern	moderno
natural	natural
near	cerca
negative	negativo
new	nuevo
next	próximo
nice	bonito
north	norte
OK	de acuerdo
old	viejo/antiguo
online	en línea
only	solamente
open	abierto
opposite	opuesto
orange	naranja
other	otro
own	propio
past	pasado
perfect	perfecto
personal	personal
pink	rosa
poor	pobre

popular	popular
positive	positivo
possible	posible
present	presente
pretty	bonita
purple	morada/púrpura
quick	rápido
quiet	tranquilo
ready	listo
real	real
red	rojo
rich	rico
right	derecho
sad	triste
same	mismo
short	corto/breve
sick	enfermo
similar	similar
slow	lento
small	pequeño
smart	inteligente
sorry	triste
south	sur
special	especial
strong	fuerte
sure	seguro
tall	alto
terrible	terrible
thirsty	sediento
tired	cansado
true	verdadero
useful	útil
warm	cálido
welcome	bienvenido

Level A1 Vocabulary

well	bien
west	oeste
white	blanco
wonderful	maravilloso
wrong	equivocado
yellow	amarillo
young	joven

A1 Adjectives Quiz

1.	aburrido		A.	beautiful
2.	oscuro		B.	dangerous
3.	amistoso		C.	married
4.	tarde		D.	near
5.	limpio		E.	poor
6.	casado		F.	tired
7.	pobre		G.	quiet
8.	hambriento		H.	wonderful
9.	tranquilo		I.	friendly
10.	enojado		J.	clean
11.	rico		K.	warm
12.	interesante		L.	useful
13.	cansado		M.	fat
14.	útil		N.	slow
15.	costoso		O.	good
16.	cálido		P.	rich
17.	gordo		Q.	bored
18.	cerca		R.	open
19.	maravilloso		S.	expensive
20.	lento		T.	late
21.	abierto		U.	long
22.	hermosa		V.	dark
23.	largo		W.	interesting
24.	bueno		X.	hungry
25.	peligroso		Y.	angry

Answer Key

1. Q
2. V
3. I
4. T
5. J
6. C
7. E
8. X
9. G
10. Y
11. P
12. W
13. F
14. L
15. S
16. K
17. M
18. D
19. H
20. N
21. R
22. A
23. U
24. O
25. B

A1 Adverbs

English Word	Spanish Translation
about	acerca/sobre
above	arriba/por encima de
across	a través
again	de nuevo/otra vez
ago	atrás/antes
also	además/también
always	siempre
around	alrededor
away	fuera
back	atrás
behind	detrás
below	abajo/debajo
down	abajo
downstairs	abajo de las escaleras
each	cada
early	temprano
east	este
else	más
enough	suficiente
even	incluso
ever	alguna vez
far	lejos
fast	rápido
hard	duro
here	aquí
home	casa/hogar
how	cómo
however	sin embargo/de todos modos
in	en

just	solo
late	tarde
later	más tarde
left	izquierda
long	largo
lot	mucho
maybe	quizás/tal vez
more	más
most	el más
much	mucho
near	cerca
never	nunca
next	próximo
north	norte
not	no
now	ahora
o'clock	en punto
off	apagado
often	a menudo
OK	de acuerdo
on	sobre
once	una vez
online	en línea
only	solamente
opposite	opuesto
out	fuera
outside	afuera
over	sobre
pretty	bastante
probably	probablemente
quickly	con rapidez
quite	bastante
really	de verdad

right	derecho
same	mismo
so	asi
sometimes	algunas veces
soon	pronto
south	sur
still	todavía
then	después/entonces
there	allí
through	a través de
today	hoy
together	juntos
tomorrow	mañana
tonight	esta noche
too	también/demasiado
twice	dos veces
under	debajo
up	hasta/arriba
upstairs	piso de arriba
usually	usualmente
very	muy
well	bien/pues
west	oeste
when	cuándo
where	dónde
why	por qué
yesterday	el dia de ayer

A1 Adverbs Quiz

1.	abajo	A.	far
2.	lejos	B.	in
3.	además/también	C.	just
4.	duro	D.	now
5.	una vez	E.	always
6.	quizás	F.	quite
7.	probablemente	G.	often
8.	bastante	H.	also
9.	siempre	I.	today
10.	derecho	J.	down
11.	allí	K.	soon
12.	a menudo	L.	under
13.	en	M.	once
14.	muy	N.	hard
15.	bien/pues	O.	maybe
16.	solo	P.	however
17.	Sin embargo	Q.	long
18.	El día de ayer	R.	probably
19.	ahora	S.	right
20.	bajo	T.	behind
21.	hoy	U.	well
22.	atrás	V.	very
23.	pronto	W.	yesterday
24.	largo	X.	there
25.	cada	Y.	each

Answer Key

1. J
2. A
3. H
4. N
5. M
6. O
7. R
8. F
9. E
10. S
11. X
12. G
13. B
14. V
15. U
16. C
17. P
18. W
19. D
20. L
21. I
22. T
23. K
24. Q
25. Y

A1 Special Words

Exclamations

English Word	Spanish Translation
bye	adiós
hey	oye
hi	hola
no	no
oh	oh
OK	de acuerdo
please	por favor
sorry	perdón
thanks	gracias
welcome	bienvenido
well	bien
yeah	sí
yes	si
hello	hola
goodbye	adiós

Numbers

English Word	Spanish Translation
one	uno
two	dos
second (next after the first)	segundo
three	tres
third	tercero
four	cuatro
fourth	cuarto

fifth	quinto
five	cinco
six	seis
seven	siete
eight	ocho
nine	nueve
ten	diez
eleven	once
twelve	doce
thirteen	trece
fourteen	catorce
fifteen	quince
sixteen	dieciséis
seventeen	diecisiete
eighteen	dieciocho
nineteen	diecinueve
twenty	veinte
thirty	treinta
forty	cuarenta
fifty	cincuenta
sixty	sesenta
seventy	setenta
eighty	ochenta
ninety	noventa
hundred	cien
thousand	mil
million	millón

Pronouns

English Word	Spanish Translation
all	todos
another	otro
any	ninguna/cualquier

anyone	alguien
anything	cualquier cosa
both	ambos
each	cada
enough	suficiente
everybody	todos
everyone	todo el mundo
everything	todo
few	pocos
he	él
her	ella/su
him	él
I	yo
it	eso/lo
lot	lote/mucho
me	mi
no one	ninguno
nobody	nadie
nothing	nada
one	uno
other	otro
own	propio
same	mismo
she	ella
some	algunos
somebody	alguien
someone	alguien
something	algo
that	que
them	ellos
they	ellos
us	nosotros
we	nosotros

what	qué
when	cuándo
which	cuáles/cuál
who	quién
you	usted
yourself	usted mismo

Prepositions

English Word	Spanish Translation
about	sobre/acerca
above	arriba
across	a través de
after	después
around	alrededor
as	como
at	en
before	antes
behind	detrás
below	abajo
between	entre
by	por
down	abajo
during	durante
for	por/para
from	desde
into	en
like (similar)	como/parecido/semejante
near	cerca
next to	junto a
of	de
off	apagado
on	en/sobre
opposite	opuesto

out	fuera
outside	afuera
over	sobre
past	pasado
through	a través de
to	a/para
under	bajo
until	hasta
up	hasta/arriba
with	con
without	sin

Determiners

English Word	Spanish Translation
little	pequeño
each	cada
every	todos/cada
his	su
its	su
last	último
lot	lote
my	mi
no	no
one	uno
our	nuestro
second (next after the first)	segundo
some	algunos
that	ese
their	su
what	qué
which	cuales
your	tu

enough	suficiente
her	su
few	pocos
first	primero
half	medio
many	muchos
more	más
most	el más
much	mucho
this	este

Conjunctions

English Word	Spanish Translation
or	o
and	y
because	porque
but	pero
if	si
so	por tanto/por consiguiente
than	que
that	que/en que
until	hasta que
when	cuándo
where	dónde

A1 Vocabulary Final Exam

1. ver	A. map
2. factura	B. talk
3. recordar	C. fat
4. peligroso	D. long
5. lejos	E. have
6. casa	F. rich
7. tener	G. bill
8. interesante	H. quite
9. bastante	I. dangerous
10. tío	J. today
11. util	K. remember
12. hoy	L. know
13. saber	M. interesting
14. cansado	N. far
15. arroz	O. in
16. esperar	P. egg
17. enojado	Q. learn
18. duro	R. always
19. en	S. tired
20. huevo	T. hard
21. hambriento	U. bring
22. ahora	V. soon
23. conducir	W. often
24. pronto	X. angry
25. hablar	Y. right
26. largo	Z. week
27. sin embargo	AA. see
28. a menudo	BB. yesterday
29. nombre	CC. behind
30. gordo	DD. under
31. siempre	EE. rice
32. rico	FF. however

33. trabajo	GG. now
34. cálido	HH. drive
35. derecho	II. hungry
36. el día de ayer	JJ. warm
37. mapa	KK. uncle
38. traer	LL. useful
39. atrás	MM. wait
40. aprender	NN. house
41. bajo	OO. job
42. semana	PP. name
43. ir	QQ. kitchen
44. tarde	RR. do
45. necesidad	SS. poor
46. una vez	TT. probably
47. hacer	UU. need
48. probablemente	VV. once
49. pobre	WW. late
50. cocina	XX. go

Answer Key

1.	AA	26.	D
2.	G	27.	FF
3.	K	28.	W
4.	I	29.	PP
5.	N	30.	C
6.	NN	31.	R
7.	E	32.	F
8.	M	33.	OO
9.	H	34.	JJ
10.	KK	35.	Y
11.	LL	36.	BB
12.	J	37.	A
13.	L	38.	U
14.	S	39.	CC
15.	EE	40.	Q
16.	MM	41.	DD
17.	X	42.	Z
18.	T	43.	XX
19.	O	44.	WW
20.	P	45.	UU
21.	II	46.	VV
22.	GG	47.	RR
23.	HH	48.	TT
24.	V	49.	SS
25.	B	50.	Q

Level A2 Vocabulary

Level A2, the second level of the CEFR, is considered the elementary level. One is still a beginner at this level, but has advanced beyond Level A1. According to the official CEFR guidelines, someone at the A2 level in Spanish:

- Can understand sentences and frequently used expressions related to areas of most immediate relevance (e.g. very basic personal and family information, shopping, local geography, employment) (Council of Europe 2022).
- Can communicate in simple and routine tasks requiring a simple and direct exchange of information on familiar and routine matters (Council of Europe 2022).
- Can describe in simple terms aspects of his/her background, immediate environment and matters in areas of immediate need (Council of Europe 2022).

A2 Nouns

English Word	Spanish Translation
ability	habilidad
accident	accidente
advantage	ventaja
adventure	aventura
advertisement	anuncio
advertising	publicidad
airline	aerolínea
alternative	alternativa
amount	monto/cantidad
ankle	tobillo
app	aplicación
appearance	apariencia
architect	arquitecto
architecture	arquitectura
argument	argumento
army	ejército
arrangement	acuerdo
assistant	asistente
athlete	atleta
attack	ataque
attention	atención
audience	audiencia
author	autor
average	promedio
award	premio
background	antecedentes/fondo
bean	frijol
bear (animal)	oso

beef	carne de res
behavior	comportamiento
belt	cinturón
benefit	beneficio
best	mejor
biology	biología
birth	nacimiento
bit	bit/poco
blank	blanco
block	cuadra/bloque
blood	sangre
board	tablero/bordo
bone	hueso
boss	patrón/jefe
bottom	abajo
bowl	cuenco
brain	cerebro
bridge	puente
brush	cepillo
businessman	empresario
button	botón
camp	campamento
camping	cámping
campus	instalaciones
can	lata
candy	caramelo/dulce
care	cuidado
carpet	alfombra/moqueta
cartoon	dibujos animados
case	caso
cash	dinero en efectivo
cause	causa
celebrity	celebridad
cell	celda/celular

century	siglo
chain	cadena
chance	oportunidad
character	personaje/carácter
charity	caridad
chat	charla
check	cheque/cuenta
chef	cocinero
chemistry	química
chick	polluelo/pollito
chip	chip
choice	elección
church	iglesia
cigarette	cigarrillo
circle	círculo
clerk	secretario
climate	clima
closet	armario
clothing	ropa
cloud	nube
coach	entrenador
coast	costa
code	código
colleague	colega
column	columna
comedy	comedia
comment	comentario
community	comunidad
competition	competencia
condition	condición
conference	conferencia
context	contexto
continent	continente

control	control
cook	cocinero
cookie	galleta
copy	copia
corner	esquina
couple	pareja
credit	crédito
crime	delito/crimen
criminal	delincuente
cross	cruz
crowd	multitud/muchedumbre
cycle	ciclo
danger	peligro
dark	oscuro
data	datos
death	muerte
decision	decisión
degree	grado
dentist	dentista
department	departamento
desert	desierto
designer	diseñador
dessert	postre
detective	detective
device	dispositivo/aparato
diary	diario
direction	dirección
director	director
disaster	desastre
discovery	descubrimiento
discussion	discusión
disease	enfermedad
distance	distancia
document	documento

download	descargar
downtown	centro
drama	drama
drawing	dibujo
dream	sueño
drive (computer)	unidad
driving	conducción/manejo
drug	droga
duck	pato
earth	tierra
education	educación
effect	efecto
electricity	electricidad
elevator	ascensor
employee	empleado
employer	empleador
ending	finalizando
energy	energía
engine	motor
engineer	ingeniero
environment	ambiente
equipment	equipo
error	error
essay	ensayo
evidence	evidencia
experience	experiencia
experiment	experimento
expert	experto
explanation	explicación
expression	expresión
factor	factor
factory	fábrica
fan	admirador

farming	agricultura
fashion	moda
fat	grasa
fear	miedo
feature	rasgo/característica
female	mujer
fever	fiebre
fiction	ficción
field	campo
fight	lucha/pelea
figure	figura
film	película
final	final
finger	dedo
finish	acabado/final
fishing	pesca
flu	gripe
fly	mosca
flying	volador/vuelo
focus	foco
forest	bosque
fork	tenedor
frog	rana
furniture	mueble
gallery	galería
gap	brecha
garbage	basura
gas	gas/gasolina
gate	portón/puerta
gift	regalo
goal	meta
god	dios
gold	oro
golf	golf

good	bueno
government	gobierno
grass	césped/hierba
grocery	tienda de comestibles
ground	tierra/suelo
guest	invitado/huésped
guide	guía
gun	pistola
guy	chico
habit	hábito
hall	salón/pasillo
headache	dolor de cabeza
heart	corazón
heat	calor
height	altura
hero	héroe
hill	cerro/colina
hit	golpe
hockey	hockey
hole	agujero
holiday	vacación
hope	esperanza
human	humano
illness	enfermedad
image	imagen
increase	incrementar
individual	individual
industry	industria
injury	lesión
insect	insecto
inside	en el interior
instruction	instrucción
instructor	instructor

instrument	instrumento
introduction	introducción
invention	invención
invitation	invitación
item	artículo
jam	mermelada/atasco
jazz	jazz
jewelry	joyas
joke	broma
journalist	periodista
jump	salto
kid	niño
kilometer	kilómetro
king	rey
knee	rodilla
knife	cuchillo
knowledge	conocimiento
lab	laboratorio
lady	dama
lake	lago
lamp	lámpara
laptop	ordenador portátil
last	último
laughter	risa
law	ley
lawyer	abogado
leader	líder
learning	aprendiendo
lecture	conferencia
lemon	limón
level	nivel
lifestyle	estilo de vida
link	enlace
listener	oyente

lock	cerrar con llave
look	mirada/vistazo
luck	suerte
mail	correo
male	masculino
manager	gerente
manner	manera
mark	marca
material	material
math	matemáticas
mathematics	matemáticas
matter	materia
mayor	alcalde
media	medios de comunicación
medicine	medicina
memory	memoria
metal	metal
method	método
middle	medio
mind	mente
mirror	espejo
miss	señorita
monkey	mono
moon	luna
motorcycle	motocicleta
movement	movimiento
musician	músico
nature	naturaleza
neck	cuello
need	necesidad
network	red
noise	ruido
notice	aviso

novel	novedoso
nut	nuez
offer	oferta
officer	oficial
oil	aceite/petróleo
opportunity	oportunidad
option	opción
organization	organización
oven	horno
owner	propietario
pain	dolor
painter	pintor
palace	palacio
parking	estacionamiento
passenger	pasajero
patient	paciente
pattern	modelo/patrón
peace	paz
penny	centavo
percent	por ciento
permission	permiso
personality	personalidad
pet	mascota
physics	física
pilot	piloto
planet	planeta
plastic	plastico
plate	placa
platform	plataforma
pocket	bolsillo
pollution	contaminación
pop	estallido
population	población
position	posición

possession	posesión
possibility	posibilidad
poster	póster
power	poder/energíá/potencia
president	presidente
printer	impresora
prison	prisión
prize	premio
process	proceso
professor	profesor
profile	perfil
progress	progreso
promise	promesa
public	público
purpose	objetivo
quality	calidad
quantity	cantidad
queen	reina
race (competition)	carrera
railroad	ferrocarril
rate	velocidad/tarifa
reception	recepción
recipe	receta
record	registro
recording	grabación
refrigerator	refrigerador
region	región
relationship	relación
reply	respuesta
reporter	reportero
request	solicitud
research	investigar
researcher	investigador

response	respuesta
rest (remaining part)	resto
rest (sleep/relax)	descanso
review	revisión
ride	paseo
ring	anillo
rock (music)	música rock
rock (stone)	roca/piedra
role	papel/role
roof	techo
route	ruta
run	corrida/carrera
runner	corredor
sailing	navegación
salary	sueldo
sale	rebaja
sauce	salsa
saw	sierra
scene	escena
schedule	horario/calendario
score	puntaje/puntuación
screen	pantalla
sea	mar
search	búsqueda
season	temporada
seat	asiento/sede/silla
secret	secreto
secretary	secretario
sense	sentido
series	serie
service	servicio
shape	forma
sheet	hoja
ship	barco/navio/embarcacion

shoulder	hombro
shout	grito
side	lado
sign	signo
silver	plata
single	único/individuo/soltero
sir	señor
site	sitio
size	talla/tamaño
ski	esquí
skin	piel
sky	cielo
sleep	sueño
smartphone	teléfono inteligente
smell	olor/olfato
smile	sonrisa
smoke	humo
sneaker	zapatilla de deporte
soap	jabón
soccer	fútbol
society	sociedad
sock	calcetín
soldier	soldado
solution	solución
sort	tipo
source	fuente
speaker	orador/altavoz/hablante
speech	discurso/habla
speed	velocidad
spider	araña
spoon	cuchara
square	cuadrado
stage	etapa

stair	escalera
stamp	estampilla
start	comienzo
state	estado
stay	estancia/visita
step	paso
stomach	estómago
stone	piedra/roca
storm	tormenta
stove	estufa
strategy	estrategia
stress	estrés
structure	estructura
subway	subterraneo
suggestion	sugerencia
suit	traje
support	soporte
surprise	sorpresa
survey	encuesta
symbol	símbolo
system	sistema
tablet	tableta
talk	conversación/plática
target	objetivo
task	tarea
taste	sabor
teaching	enseñanza
technology	tecnología
teeth	dientes
temperature	temperatura
term	término/plazo
thief	ladrón
thinking	pensando
thought	pensamiento

tie	corbata/lazo
tip	propina
tool	herramienta
top	parte superior/cima
tour	gira
tourism	turismo
towel	toalla
tower	torre
toy	juguete
track	pista
tradition	tradicion
training	capacitación
transportation	transportación
trash	basura
traveler	viajero
triangle	triángulo
trouble	problema
twin	mellizo/gemelo
understanding	comprensión
uniform	uniforme
unit	unidad
use	uso
user	usuario
valley	valle
variety	variedad
vehicle	vehículo
view	vista
village	pueblo
virus	virus
voice	voz
wait	espera
war	guerra
wash	lavado

washing	lavado
wave	onda/ola
web	web
wedding	boda
weight	peso
welcome	bienvenida
wheel	rueda
wind	viento
winner	ganador
wish	deseo
wood	madera

A2 Nouns Quiz

1.	carne de res	A.	advantaje
2.	hueso	B.	can
3.	desierto	C.	fork
4.	promedio	D.	hope
5.	explicación	E.	beef
6.	brecha	F.	nut
7.	lata	G.	percent
8.	tenedor	H.	pop
9.	esperanza	I.	bone
10.	ventaja	J.	quantity
11.	manera	K.	source
12.	salto	L.	amount
13.	por ciento	M.	cook
14.	comportamiento	N.	survey
15.	fuente	O.	cause
16.	cantidad	P.	wood
17.	encuesta	Q.	behavior
18.	habilidad	R.	manner
19.	madera	S.	average
20.	estallido	T.	jump
21.	rasgo	U.	gap
22.	nuez	V.	desert
23.	cocinero	W.	feature
24.	monto	X.	explanation
25.	causa	Y.	ability

Answer Key

1. E
2. I
3. V
4. S
5. X
6. U
7. B
8. C
9. D
10. A
11. R
12. T
13. G
14. Q
15. K
16. J
17. N
18. Y
19. P
20. H
21. W
22. F
23. M
24. L
25. O

A2 Verbs

English Word	Spanish Translation
accept	aceptar
achieve	lograr
act	actuar
advertise	anunciar/hacer publicidad
affect	afectar
allow	permitir
analyze	analizar
appear	aparecer
apply	solicitar
argue	discutir
arrange	arreglar/organizar
attack	atacar
attend	asistir
avoid	evitar
beat	vencer/derrotar/latir
behave	comportarse
belong	pertenecer
blow	soplar
boil	hervir
book	libro
borrow	tomar prestado
brush	cepillar
burn	quemar
camp	acampar
care	cuidar/importar
catch	captura
cause	causar
celebrate	celebrar

chat	charlar
circle	rodear
collect	recopilar/recoger
communicate	comunicar
compete	competir
complain	quejarse
connect	conectar
consider	considerar
contain	contener
continue	seguir/continuar
control	controlar
copy	copiar
count	contar
cover	cubrir
cross	cruzar
cry	llorar
deal	tratar
depend	depender
destroy	destruir
develop	desarrollar
disagree	discrepar
disappear	desaparecer
discover	descubrir
double	doblar
download	descargar
dream	soñar
drop	soltar/caer
dry	secar
earn	ganar
employ	emplear
enter	ingresar/entrar
exist	existir
expect	esperar/suponer
express	rápido

fail	fallar
farm	cosechar/cultivar
feed	alimentar
fell	cayó
fight	pelear
film	filmar
fire	disparar/incendiar
fish	pescar
fit	encajar
fix	arreglar
focus	enfocar
greet	saludar
grew	creció
guide	guiar
has	tiene
heat	calentar
hide	ocultar
hit	pegar/golpear
hold	sostener/mantener
hurt	lastimar
identify	identificar
increase	incrementar
invent	inventar
invite	invitar
involve	involucrar
joke	bromear
jump	saltar
kill	matar
knock	golpear
land	aterrizar
last (taking time)	durar
lead	liderar/conducir
lend	prestar

lift	levantar/elevar
light (from the sun/a lamp)	iluminar
link	enlazar/vincular
lock	cerrar con llave
mail	enviar por correo
manage	gestionar/administrar
mark	marcar
marry	casarse
matter	importar
mention	mencionar
might	podría
notice	notar/observar
offer	ofrecer
organize	organizar
own	poseer
pack	empacar
pass	pasar/aprobar
perform	actuar/realizar
photograph	fotografiar
pick	recoger/escoger
plant	plantar/sembrar
please	complacer/agradar
predict	predecir
present	presentar
prevent	prevenir
print	imprimir
produce	producir
progress	progresar
promise	prometer
pronounce	pronunciar
protect	proteger
provide	proveer
publish	publicar
pull	tirar

push	empujar
question	preguntar/interrogar
race (competition)	correr/competir
raise	aumentar
reach	alcanzar
react	reaccionar
realize	darse cuenta de
receive	recibir
recognize	reconocer
recommend	recomendar
record	grabar/registrar
recycle	reciclar
reduce	reducir
refer	referirse
refuse	negar
remove	retirar
repair	reparar
replace	reemplazar
reply	responder
report	reporter/informar
research	investigar
respond	responder
rest (sleep/relax)	descansar
review	revisar/reseñar
ring	sonar/llamar
rise	aumentar
sail	navegar
save	ahorrar
score	marcar/calificar
search	buscar
seem	parecer
serve	servir
shake	sacudir

shout	gritar
shut	cerrar
sign	firmar
singing	cantando
ski	esquiar
smell	oler
smile	sonreír
smoke	fumar
solve	resolver
star	protagonizar
steal	robar
stress	estresar
succeed	triunfar
suggest	sugerir
support	apoyar
suppose	suponer
surprise	sorprender
taste	probar
text	textear
throw	tirar/lanzar
tie	atar/empatar
touch	tocar
train	entrenar
wish	desear
worry	preocuparse

A2 Verbs Quiz

1.	contar	A.	greet
2.	hervir	B.	pull
3.	saludar	C.	raise
4.	levantar/elevar	D.	advertise
5.	tirar	E.	manage
6.	aumentar	F.	might
7.	responder	G.	predict
8.	anunciar	H.	appear
9.	tocar	I.	count
10.	gestionar	J.	avoid
11.	marcar	K.	burn
12.	podría	L.	contain
13.	oferta	M.	double
14.	predecir	N.	boil
15.	empujar	O.	hide
16.	aparecer	P.	invite
17.	evitar	Q.	pack
18.	contener	R.	compete
19.	doblar	S.	push
20.	desarrollar	T.	offer
21.	ocultar	U.	mark
22.	invitar	V.	touch
23.	embalar	W.	reply
24.	quemar	X.	lift
25.	competir	Y.	develop

Answer Key

1.   I
2.   N
3.   A
4.   X
5.   B
6.   C
7.   W
8.   D
9.   V
10. E
11. U
12. F
13. T
14. G
15. S
16. H
17. J
18. L
19. M
20. Y
21. O
22. P
23. Q
24. K
25. R

A2 Adjectives

English Word	Spanish Translation
light (not heavy)	ligero
able	capaz
active	activo
adult	adulto
alive	vivo
all right	está bien
alone	sólo
ancient	antiguo
asleep	dormido
assistant	asistente
attractive	atractivo
available	disponible
average	promedio
awful	horrible
back	de vuelta/trasero
based	basado
blank	blanco
bottom	del fondo
bright	brillante/luminoso
brilliant	brillante
broken	roto
careful	cuidado
certain	determinado/cierto
classical	clásico
clear	claro
close	cercano/proximo
closed	cerrado
comfortable	cómodo

connected	conectado
crazy	loco
creative	creativo
crowded	saturado
curly	ondulado
daily	diario
dead	muerto
deep	profundo
digital	digital
direct	directo
distant	distante
divorced	divorciado
double	doble
downstairs	abajo
downtown	centro
dry	seco
electric	eléctrico
electrical	eléctrico
electronic	electrónico
empty	vacío
enormous	enorme
everyday	cada día
exact	exacto
excellent	excelente
expert	experto
extreme	extremo
fair	justo
female	mujer
fine	fina
fit	en forma
flat	plano
flying	volante
following	siguiente
foreign	extranjero

formal	formal
fresh	fresco
fun	divertido/diversión
further	más lejos
future	futuro
general	general
gold	oro
heavy	pesado
helpful	servicial
home	casa
huge	enorme
human	humano
hurt	lastimar
ideal	ideal
ill	enfermo
impossible	imposible
included	incluido
incredible	increíble
independent	independiente
individual	individual
informal	informal
inside	en el interior
intelligent	inteligente
international	internacional
later	más tarde
lazy	perezoso
likely	probable
lost	perdido
loud	fuerte
low	bajo
lucky	suerte
major	mayor
male	masculino

medical	médico
middle	medio
missing	desaparecidos
musical	musical
narrow	angosto/estrecho
national	nacional
necessary	necesario
nervous	nervioso
noisy	ruidoso
normal	normal
ordinary	común
original	original
outside	afuera
particular	particular/especial
percent	por ciento
physical	físico
plastic	plástico
pleased	satisfecho
polite	educado
professional	profesional
recent	reciente
regular	regular
round	ronda
rude	grosero/brusco
safe	seguro
scared	asustado
scary	asustadizo
secret	secreto
separate	separado
serious	grave
shut	cerrado
silver	plata
simple	sencilla
single	único/solo

social	social
soft	suave
specific	específico
square	cuadrado
straight	derecho/recto
strange	extraño
stupid	estúpido
successful	exitoso
surprised	sorprendido
surprising	sorprendente
sweet	dulce
teenage	adolescente
these	éstos
thick	grueso
thin	delgado
top	parte superior
toy	juguete
traditional	tradicional
twin	mellizo/gemelo
typical	típico
underground	bajo tierra
unhappy	infeliz
united	unido
unusual	inusual
upstairs	piso de arriba
usual	habitual
weak	débil
wet	húmedo/mojado
whole	todo
wide	ancho/amplio
wild	salvaje
wooden	de madera
working	trabajando

worried	preocupado
worse	peor
worst	el peor

A2 Adjectives Quiz

1.	el peor	A.	wooden
2.	de madera	B.	united
3.	habitual	C.	separate
4.	unido	D.	pleased
5.	delgado	E.	crazy
6.	suave	F.	likely
7.	separado	G.	clear
8.	de miedo	H.	worst
9.	ronda	I.	alone
10.	educado	J.	deep
11.	satisfecho	K.	enormous
12.	ruidoso	L.	alive
13.	angosto	M.	scary
14.	probable	N.	available
15.	enfermo	O.	asleep
16.	mujer	P.	ancient
17.	enorme	Q.	thin
18.	profundo	R.	female
19.	loco	S.	ill
20.	claro	T.	narrow
21.	antiguo	U.	round
22.	solo	V.	polite
23.	vivo	W.	noisy
24.	disponible	X.	soft
25.	dormido	Y.	usual

Answer Key

1. H
2. A
3. Y
4. B
5. Q
6. X
7. C
8. M
9. U
10. V
11. D
12. W
13. T
14. F
15. S
16. R
17. K
18. J
19. E
20. G
21. P
22. I
23. L
24. N
25. O

A2 Adverbs

English Word	Spanish Translation
actually	realmente
after	después
all	todos
all right	está bien
almost	casi
alone	solo
along	a lo largo de
already	ya
any	ninguna/cualquier
anymore	ya no
anyway	de todos modos
anywhere	en cualquier sitio
as	como
badly	gravemente
before	antes
best	el mejor
better	mejor
between	entre
carefully	cuidadosamente
certainly	seguramente
clearly	claramente
completely	completamente
correctly	correctamente
definitely	definitivamente
differently	diferentemente
downtown	centro
easily	fácilmente
either	cualquiera

especially	especialmente
everywhere	en todas partes
exactly	exactamente
extremely	extremadamente
finally	finalmente
first	primero
fortunately	por suerte
forward	adelante
free	gratis
half	medio
happily	felizmente
high	elevado
immediately	inmediatamente
inside	en el interior
instead	en cambio
last	último
least	el menos
less	menos
little	pequeño
loud	fuerte
loudly	ruidosamente
low	bajo
mostly	principalmente
nearly	por poco
normally	normalmente
nowhere	en ningún lugar
overseas	exterior
past	pasado
percent	porciento
perhaps	tal vez/quizás
quietly	silencioso
rather	en lugar de
recently	recientemente
round	alrededor

sadly	tristemente
second (next after the first)	en segundo lugar
slowly	lentamente
somewhere	algun lado
straight	directamente
suddenly	repentinamente/de repente
sure	seguro
underground	bajo tierra
unfortunately	desafortunadamente
yet	aún/todavía

A2 Adverbs Quiz

1.	seguro	A.	loud
2.	algún lado	B.	little
3.	repentinamente	C.	free
4.	pasado	D.	exactly
5.	exterior	E.	somewhere
6.	bajo	F.	downtown
7.	fuerte	G.	clearly
8.	menos	H.	better
9.	pequeño	I.	actually
10.	último	J.	all
11.	medio	K.	already
12.	gratis	L.	certainly
13.	exactamente	M.	suddenly
14.	centro	N.	either
15.	claramente	O.	as
16.	mejor	P.	recently
17.	como	Q.	overseas
18.	ya	R.	almost
19.	casi	S.	anymore
20.	todos	T.	half
21.	realmente	U.	past
22.	ya no	V.	last
23.	seguramente	W.	less
24.	cualquiera	X.	low
25.	hace poco	Y.	sure

Level A2 Vocabulary

Answer Key

1. Y
2. E
3. M
4. U
5. Q
6. X
7. A
8. W
9. B
10. V
11. T
12. C
13. D
14. F
15. G
16. H
17. O
18. K
19. R
20. J
21. I
22. S
23. L
24. N
25. P

93

A2 Special Words

Exclamations

English Word	Spanish Translation
ah	ah
wow	guau

Numbers

English Word	Spanish Translation
billion	mil millones/un billón
zero	cero

Pronouns

English Word	Spanish Translation
anybody	cualquiera
anywhere	en cualquier sitio
double	doble
hers	suyo
herself	sí misma
himself	él mismo
his	su
itself	sí mismo
mine (belongs to me)	mio
myself	yo mismo
none	ninguno
ourselves	nosotros mismos
several	varios
somewhere	algun lado
such	que

themselves	ellos mismos
whose	cuyo
yours	tuya

Prepositions

English Word	Spanish Translation
according to	de acuerdo a
against	en contra
along	a lo largo de
among	entre
except	excepto
including	incluido
inside	en el interior
onto	sobre
per	por
since	desde
toward	hacia

Determiners

English Word	Spanish Translation
several	varios
such	tal/semejante
whose	cuyo
either	cualquiera
least	el menos
less	menos
neither	ni

Nothing But Beginner Vocab: Spanish Edition

Conjunctions

English Word	Spanish Translation
after	después
although	aunque
as	como
before	antes
since	desde
while	mientras

A2 Vocabulary Final Exam

1. lata	A. beef
2. saludar	B. hide
3. suave	C. pull
4. separado	D. female
5. cantidad	E. crazy
6. hervir	F. ill
7. solo	G. alive
8. encuesta	H. can
9. ocultar	I. greet
10. angosto	J. deep
11. mujer	K. bone
12. monto	L. free
13. tirar	M. less
14. ruidoso	N. downtown
15. loco	O. quantity
16. hueso	P. separate
17. empujar	Q. exactly
18. enfermo	R. gap
19. gratis	S. either
20. menos	T. certainly
21. centro	U. push
22. comportamiento	V. almost
23. marcar	W. amount
24. profundo	X. better
25. exterior	Y. last
26. exactamente	Z. survey
27. último	AA. mark
28. brecha	BB. ancient
29. gestionar	CC. ability
30. unido	DD. might
31. cualquiera	EE. overseas
32. mejor	FF. available

33. antiguo
34. madera
35. podría
36. vivo
37. seguramente
38. casi
39. disponible
40. habilidad
41. responder
42. carne de res
43. fuente
44. levanter/elevar
45. educado
46. ya
47. pasado
48. manera
49. doblar
50. de miedo

GG. boil
HH. reply
II. united
JJ. noisy
KK. narrow
LL. manage
MM. alone
NN. soft
OO. wood
PP. behavior
QQ. manner
RR. lift
SS. already
TT. past
UU. source
VV. scary
WW. polite
XX. double

Answer Key

1.	H	26.	Q
2.	I	27.	Y
3.	NN	28.	R
4.	P	29.	LL
5.	O	30.	II
6.	GG	31.	S
7.	MM	32.	X
8.	Z	33.	BB
9.	B	34.	OO
10.	KK	35.	DD
11.	D	36.	G
12.	W	37.	T
13.	C	38.	V
14.	JJ	39.	FF
15.	E	40.	CC
16.	K	41.	HH
17.	U	42.	A
18.	F	43.	UU
19.	L	44.	RR
20.	M	45.	WW
21.	N	46.	SS
22.	PP	47.	TT
23.	AA	48.	QQ
24.	J	49.	XX
25.	EE	50.	VV

Level B1 Vocabulary

English level B1 is the third level of English in the Common European Framework of Reference (CEFR). This level is considered "intermediate", and indeed, that is the official level description in the CEFR. At this level, students are beyond the basics but they are still not able to work or study exclusively in Spanish. According to the official CEFR guidelines, someone at the B1 level in Spanish:

- Can understand the main points of clear standard input on familiar matters regularly encountered in work, school, leisure, etc. (Council of Europe 2022).
- Can deal with most situations likely to arise whilst travelling in an area where the language is spoken (Council of Europe 2022).
- Can produce simple connected text on topics which are familiar or of personal interest (Council of Europe 2022).
- Can describe experiences and events, dreams, hopes & ambitions and briefly give reasons and explanations for opinions and plans (Council of Europe 2022).

B1 Nouns

English Word	Spanish Translation
access	acceso
account	cuenta
achievement	logro
act	acto
ad	anuncio
addition	suma
administration	administración
agent	agente
agreement	convenio
aim	apuntar
alarm	alarma
album	álbum
alcohol	alcohol
ambition	ambición
analysis	análisis
announcement	anuncio
application	solicitud/aplicación
appointment	cita
arrest	detención
arrival	llegada
assignment	asignación
atmosphere	atmósfera
attitude	actitud
attraction	atracción
authority	autoridad
balance	equilibrio/saldo/balance
ban	prohibición
bank (river)	banco

base	base
basis	bases
battery	batería
battle	batalla
beauty	belleza
bee	abeja
belief	creencia
bell	campana
bend	curva
better	mejor
bite	mordida
bomb	bomba
border	frontera
branch	sucursal/rama
brand	marca
breath	aliento
breathing	respiración
bride	novia
bubble	burbuja
cable	cable
calm	calma
campaign	campaña
candidate	candidato
cap	gorra
captain	capitán
category	categoría
ceiling	techo
celebration	celebracion
ceremony	ceremonia
champion	campeón
channel	canal
chapter	capítulo
charge	cargar
cheat	engañar

chemical	químico
chest	pecho
childhood	infancia
claim	reclamación
clause	cláusula
click	clic/tecleo
client	cliente
climb	escalada
cloth	tela/paño
clue	clave
coal	carbón
coin	moneda
collection	recopilación/colección
colony	colonia
commercial	comercial
communication	comunicación
comparison	comparación
competitor	competidor
complaint	queja
conclusion	conclusión
connection	conexión
consequence	consecuencia
consumer	consumidor
contact	contacto
container	envase
content	contenido
contrast	contraste
corn	maíz
costume	disfraz/traje
cotton	algodón
count	cuenta/recuento
countryside	campo
court	corte/tribunal/cancha

cover	cubierta/tapa
cupboard	armario
currency	divisa/moneda
curtain	cortina
custom	disfraz
cut	cortada
damage	daño
deal	trato/acuerdo
decade	década
definition	definición
departure	salida
destination	destino
development	desarrollo
diagram	diagrama
diamond	diamante
difficulty	dificultad
dirt	tierra
disadvantage	desventaja
discount	descuento
dislike	disgusto
district	distrito
documentary	documental
doubt	duda
drop	gota
drum	tambor
dust	polvo
duty	servicio/deber
earthquake	terremoto
economy	economía
edge	borde
editor	editor/redactor
effort	esfuerzo
election	elección
element	elemento

emergency	emergencia
emotion	emoción
employment	empleo
enemy	enemigo
engineering	ingeniería
entertainment	entretenimiento
entrance	entrada
entry	entrada
episode	episodio
escape	escapar
exchange	intercambio
excitement	excitación
exhibition	exhibición
exit	salida
explosion	explosión
export	exportar
extra	extra
favor	favor
fence	valla/cerca
fighting	luchando
file	expediente
fitness	aptitud física
flag	bandera
flood	inundación
flour	harina
flow	flujo
folk	gente
following	siguiente
force	fuerza
fraction	fracción
frame	marco
friendship	amistad
fuel	gasolina

function	función
fur	piel
garage	cochera
generation	generacion
gentleman	caballero
ghost	fantasma
giant	gigante
glove	guante
grade	calificación
graduate	graduado
grain	grano
growth	crecimiento
guard	guardia
happiness	felicidad
hate	odio/detesto
headline	título
heating	calefacción
helicopter	helicóptero
highlight	realce/punto culminante
highway	autopista
horror	horror
host	anfitrión
hurricane	huracán
hurry	prisa
identity	identidad
immigrant	inmigrante
impact	impacto
import	importar
importance	importancia
impression	impresión
improvement	mejora
influence	influencia
ingredient	ingrediente
instant	instantánea

intelligence	inteligencia
intention	intención
iron	plancha/hierro
issue	asunto
journal	diario
journey	viaje
judge	juez
keyboard	teclado
kick	patada/tiro
killing	asesinato
kiss	beso
knock	golpe
label	etiqueta
laboratory	laboratorio
lack	falta
layer	capa
lead	plomo
leaf	hoja
leather	cuero/piel
leisure	tiempo libre
length	longitud
lie	mentira
limit	límite
lip	labio
liquid	líquido
literature	literatura
living	viviendo
local	local
location	localización
loss	pérdida
luxury	lujo
magic	magia
magnet	imán

management	administración
marketing	marketing
marriage	casamiento
measure	medida
mention	mencionar
mess	desorden
mine (hole in the ground)	mina
mix	mezcla
mixture	mezcla
mood	estado animico
move	moverse
mud	lodo/barro
murder	asesinato
muscle	músculo
musical	musical
mystery	misterio
nail	uña/clavo
narrative	narrativo
nation	nación
native	nativo
needle	aguja
net	red
next	próximo
noon	mediodía
normal	normal
noun	sustantivo
occasion	ocasión
operation	operación
organizer	organizador
original	original
pack	paquete/envase
package	paquete
pan	sartén/pan
pass	pase/paso

passion	pasión
path	camino
payment	pago
percentage	porcentaje
performance	rendimiento
photographer	fotógrafo
photography	fotografía
pin	clavo
pipe	tubo/pipa
planning	planificación
pleasure	placer
plot	trama/parcela
poem	poema
poet	poeta
poetry	poesía
poison	veneno
policy	política
politician	político
politics	política
port	puerto
portrait	retrato
pot	maceta/olla
poverty	pobreza
powder	polvo
prayer	oración
prediction	predicción
presentation	presentación
press	prensa
pressure	presión
priest	sacerdote
prince	príncipe
princess	princesa
principal	director de escuela

printing	impresión
prisoner	prisionero
producer	productor
production	producción
profession	profesión
profit	lucro
property	propiedad
protest	protesta
pull	tracción/tirón
punishment	castigo
push	empujón
qualification	calificación
quotation	cotización
quote	cita
race (of people)	raza
racing	carreras
raise	aumento/subida
range	rango/alcance
reaction	reacción
reality	realidad
receipt	recibo
recommendation	recomendación
reference	referencia
relation	relación
relative	pariente
release	liberación
religion	religión
rent	renta/arriendo
repair	reparación
repeat	repetición
reservation	reserva
resource	recurso
respect	respeto
responsibility	responsabilidad

ring	anillo
risk	riesgo
robot	robot
roll	rollo
rope	soga/cuerda
row	fila
safety	seguridad
sail	vela
sailor	marinero
sample	muestra
sand	arena
script	texto
sculpture	escultura
security	seguridad
seed	semilla
servant	servidor
set (group)	conjunto (grupo)
setting	ajuste
sex	sexo
shake	sacudida
share	cuota/parte
shelf	estante
shell	cascarón/concha
shift	cambio
sight	vista
signal	señal
similarity	semejanza
slave	esclavo
slice	rebanada
software	software
soil	tierra/suelo
solid	sólido
spending	gasto

spirit	espíritu
spot/punto	lugar
stadium	estadio
staff	personal
standard	estándar
statistic	estadística
statue	estatua
stick (piece of wood)	palo
stranger	extraño
strength	fuerza
string	cadena/cuerda
studio	estudio
stuff	cosas
substance	sustancia
summary	resumen
supply	suministro
supporter	seguidor
surface	superficie
symptom	síntoma
tail	cola/rabo
talent	talento
tape	cinta
tax	impuesto
technique	técnica
tent	carpa
theme	temática
theory	teoría
throat	garganta
tire	neumático
toe	dedo del pie
ton	tonelada
tongue	lengua
total	total
touch	toque/tacto/contacto

trade	comercio
trainer	entrenador
translation	traducción
treatment	tratamiento
trend	tendencia
trick	truco
truth	verdad
tube	tubo
underwear	ropa interior
unemployment	desempleo
union	unión
update	actualización
value	valor
version	versión
victim	víctima
viewer	espectador
volunteer	voluntario
vote	voto/votación
warning	advertencia
waste	desperdicio
weapon	arma
while	rato/tiempo
whole	todo
will	voluntad/deseo/testamento
win	victoria
wing	ala/aleta
wonder	maravilla
wool	lana
worry	preocupación
young	joven
youth	juventud

B1 Nouns Quiz

1.	lana	A.	youth
2.	impuesto	B.	update
3.	superficie	C.	string
4.	cambio	D.	row
5.	texto	E.	release
6.	muestra	F.	press
7.	fila	G.	share
8.	liberación	H.	pin
9.	cita	I.	leisure
10.	juventud	J.	highlight
11.	prensa	K.	shift
12.	trama	L.	frame
13.	aguja	M.	poverty
14.	cuota	N.	dislike
15.	destacar	O.	wool
16.	fur	P.	measure
17.	clavo	Q.	piel
18.	espectador	R.	script
19.	marco	S.	needle
20.	medida	T.	surface
21.	disgusto	U.	plot
22.	pobreza	V.	sample
23.	tiempo libre	W.	quote
24.	actualizar	X.	tax
25.	cadena	Y.	viewer

Answer Key

1. O
2. X
3. T
4. K
5. R
6. V
7. D
8. E
9. W
10. A
11. F
12. U
13. S
14. G
15. J
16. Q
17. H
18. Y
19. L
20. P
21. N
22. M
23. I
24. B
25. C

B1 Verbs

English Word	Spanish Translation
access	acceder
admire	admirar
admit	admitir
advise	aconsejar
afford	poder pagar
age	envejecer
aim	apuntar
announce	anunciar
annoy	enojarse
apologize	pedir disculpas
appreciate	valorar
arrest	arrestar
assist	asistir
attach	adjuntar
attract	atraer
average	promedio
award	otorgar
bake	hornear
balance	equilibrar
ban	prohibir
base	basar
bend	doblar
benefit	beneficiarse
bite	morder
block	bloquear
board	abordar
bomb	bombardear
bother	molestar
brand	marcar

breathe	respirar
bury	enterrar
calm	calmar
center	centrar
charge	cargar/cobrar
cheat	engañar
claim	reclamar
clear	aclarar/limpiar
click	hacer clic
coach	entrenar
combine	combinar
comment	comentar
commit	comprometerse
concentrate	concentrarse
conclude	concluir
confirm	confirmar
confuse	confundir
consist	consistir
consume	consumer
contact	contactar
contrast	contrastar
convince	convencer
cool	enfriar
damage	dañar
define	definir
deliver	entregar
determine	determinar
did	hizo
direct	dirigir
dislike	disgustar
divide	dividir
donate	donar
done	hecho

doubt	dudar
educate	educar
empty	vaciar
encourage	alentar
entertain	entretener
escape	escapar
examine	examinar
exchange	intercambiar
excite	excitar
expand	expandir
experience	experimentar
experiment	experimentar/probar
explode	explotar
explore	explorar
export	exportar
face	enfrentar
fasten	sujetar
fear	temer
flood	inundar
flow	fluir
fold	doblar
force	forzar
frame	enmarcar/encuadrar
freeze	congelar
frighten	asustar
fry	freír
gather	reunir/recoger/recolectar
graduate	graduarse
guard	proteger
hand	entregar
hang	colgar
highlight	destacar
hire	contratar
hunt	cazar

hurry	apurarse
ignore	ignorar
impact	impactar
import	importar
indicate	indicar
influence	influenciar
injure	lesionar/herir
intend	intentar
invest	invertir
investigate	investigar
iron	planchar
judge	juzgar
kick	patear
kiss	besar
knew	sabía
label	etiquetar
lack	faltar
lay	poner/colocar
lie	mentir
limit	límitar
locate	localizar
made	hecho
market	comercializar
measure	medir
mess	ensuciar
mix	mezclar
murder	asesinar/matar
note	notar
occur	ocurrir
participate	participar
persuade	persuadir
place	poner/colocar
point	apuntar

poison	envenenar
pour	verter/servir
pray	orar
press	presionar
pretend	fingir
program	programar
promote	promover
protest	protestar
prove	probar/demostrar
punish	castigar
qualify	calificar
quit	dejar
quote	citar
reflect	reflejar
reject	rechazar
relate	relatar
release	liberar
remain	permanecer
remind	recordar
rent	alquiler
represent	representar
request	solicitar
require	requerir/exegir
respect	respetar
result	resultar
retire	jubilarse
revise	revisar
risk	arriesgar
roll	rodar
rule	mandar/gobernar
scan	escanear
separate	separar
set (put)	poner
shine	brillar

shoot	disparo
signal	señalar
sink	hundir
slice	cortar de rodajas
slow	retardar
sort	ordenar
spread	difundir
spring	saltar
state	expresar
stick (push into/attach)	pegar
store	almacenar
subtract	sustraer
suffer	sufrir
summarize	resumir
supply	suministrar
survive	sobrevivir
switch	cambiar
tax	gravar
tend	tender
tip	dar propina
tour	recorrer
trade	intercambiar
translate	traducir
transport	transportar
treat	tratar
trick	engañar
type	escribir
update	actualizar
upset	molestar
view	ver
vote	votar
warm	calentar
warn	advertir

Nothing But Beginner Vocab: Spanish Edition

waste	perder
water	regar
wave	ondear/agitar
weigh	pesar
wonder	preguntarse

B1 Verbs Quiz

1.	otorgar	A.	flood
2.	explotar	B.	locate
3.	prohibición	C.	invest
4.	inundación	D.	murder
5.	invertir	E.	occur
6.	Enterrar	F.	ban
7.	localizar	G.	roll
8.	fluir	H.	trade
9.	asesinato	I.	explode
10.	engañar	J.	vote
11.	ocurrir	K.	cheat
12.	colgar	L.	warn
13.	relatar	M.	hang
14.	convencer	N.	separate
15.	rodar	O.	poison
16.	advertir	P.	bury
17.	preguntarse	Q.	fasten
18.	intercambiar	R.	contact
19.	donar	S.	donate
20.	veneno	T.	claim
21.	sujetar	U.	convince
22.	contacto	V.	wonder
23.	separar	W.	relate
24.	reclamar	X.	flow
25.	votar	Y.	award

Answer Key

1. Y
2. I
3. F
4. A
5. C
6. P
7. B
8. X
9. D
10. K
11. E
12. M
13. W
14. U
15. G
16. L
17. V
18. H
19. S
20. O
21. Q
22. R
23. N
24. T
25. J

B1 Adjectives

English Word	Spanish Translation
academic	académico
advanced	avanzado
alcoholic	alcohólico
alternative	alternativa
amazed	asombrado
annoyed	molesto/irritado
annoying	molesto
automatic	automático
aware	consciente
basic	básico
brave	corajudo/valiente
calm	calma
careless	descuidado
central	central
cheerful	alegre
chemical	químico
clever	inteligente/listo
colored	de colores
commercial	comercial
competitive	competitivo
complex	complejo
confident	seguro
confused	confundido
continuous	continuo
convenient	conveniente
covered	cubierto
criminal	criminal/delincuente
cruel	cruel

cultural	cultural
current	actual
definite	definido
determined	determinado
disappointed	decepcionado
disappointing	decepcionante
dressed	vestido
drunk	borracho
due	adeudado
eastern	oriental
economic	económico
educated	educado
educational	educativo
effective	eficaz
embarrassed	avergonzado
embarrassing	embarazoso
engaged	comprometido
environmental	ambiental
equal	igual
essential	básico
expected	previsto
experienced	experimentado
familiar	familiar
fancy	elegante
far	lejos
fascinating	fascinante
fashionable	de moda
federal	federal
financial	financiero
fixed	fijado
folk	gente
frightened	atemorizado
frightening	atemorizante
frozen	congelado

generous	generoso
gentle	amable/suave
giant	gigante
glad	contento
global	global
grateful	agradecido
guilty	culpable
historic	histórico
historical	histórico
honest	honesto
horrible	horrible
illegal	ilegal
imaginary	imaginario
immediate	inmediato
impressive	impresionante
indirect	indirecto
indoor	interior
injured	herido/lesionado
innocent	inocente
involved	involucrado
kind (caring)	amable
latest	el último
leading	principal
legal	legal
level	nivel
liquid	líquido
live	en vivo
living	viviendo
located	situado
lonely	solitaria
mad	loco
magic	magia
medium	medio

mental	mental
mild	leve
narrative	narrativo
native	nativo
neat	ordenado
northern	del norte
nuclear	nuclear
obvious	obvio
odd	extraño
official	oficial
old-fashioned	anticuado
organized	organizado
outdoor	exterior
overseas	de ultramar
painful	doloroso
pale	pálido
peaceful	tranquilo/pacífico
pleasant	agradable
poisonous	venenoso
political	político
powerful	poderoso
practical	práctico
prepared	preparado
previous	anterior
primary	primario
private	privado
proper	correcto
proud	orgulloso
qualified	calificado
rare	raro
related	relacionado
relative	relativo
relaxed	relajado
relaxing	relajante

reliable	de confianza
religious	religioso
remote	remoto
repeated	repetido
responsible	responsable
retired	jubilado
romantic	romántico
rough	bruto
royal	real
scientific	científico
secondary	secundario
sensible	sensitivo
sexual	sexual
sharp	agudo/fuerte
shiny	brillante
shy	tímido
silent	silencioso
silly	tonto
smooth	liso
solid	sólido
southern	del sur/meridional
spicy	picante
spoken	hablado
standard	estándar
state	estatal
still	quieto
sudden	repentino
suitable	apropiado
talented	talentoso
technical	técnico
tight	ajustado
tiny	diminuto
total	total

ugly	feo
unable	incapaz
uncomfortable	incómodo
unemployed	desempleados
unfair	injusto
unlikely	improbable
unnecessary	innecesario
unpleasant	desagradable
upset	disgustado
used	usado/utilizado
valuable	valioso
various	varios
violent	violento
waste	desperdicio
western	occidental
worldwide	mundial
worth	valor
written	escrito

B1 Adjectives Quiz

1.	disgustado	A.	tiny
2.	improbable	B.	sudden
3.	valor	C.	unlikely
4.	incapaz	D.	sharp
5.	diminuto	E.	rough
6.	talentoso	F.	rare
7.	picante	G.	unable
8.	tonto	H.	pale
9.	violento	I.	mild
10.	agudo	J.	worth
11.	raro	K.	glad
12.	pálido	L.	clever
13.	ordenado	M.	amazed
14.	nivel	N.	proud
15.	contento	O.	annoying
16.	comprometido	P.	neat
17.	molesto	Q.	upset
18.	asombrado	R.	spicy
19.	gente	S.	basic
20.	básico	T.	engaged
21.	inteligente	U.	silly
22.	leve	V.	folk
23.	orgulloso	W.	level
24.	bruto	X.	talented
25.	repentino	Y.	violent

Answer Key

1. Q
2. C
3. J
4. G
5. A
6. X
7. R
8. U
9. Y
10. D
11. F
12. H
13. P
14. W
15. K
16. T
17. O
18. M
19. V
20. S
21. L
22. I
23. N
24. E
25. B

B1 Adverbs

English Word	Spanish Translation
absolutely	absolutamente
ahead	adelante
apart	aparte
approximately	aproximadamente
automatically	automáticamente
backward	hacia atrás
by	por
cheap	barato
close	cerca
currently	en la actualidad
daily	diario
deep	profundo
direct	directo
directly	directamente
effectively	efectivamente
equally	igualmente
eventually	finalmente
extra	extra
fairly	equitativamente
forever	para siempre
frequently	frecuentemente
further	más lejos
generally	generalmente
hardly	difícilmente
heavily	fuertemente
highly	muy
incredibly	increíblemente
indeed	por supuesto

indoors	adentro
live	en vivo
mainly	principalmente
meanwhile	entretanto
naturally	naturalmente
necessarily	necesariamente
neither	ni
nor	ni
obviously	obviamente
originally	originalmente
outdoors	al aire libre
particularly	particularmente
perfectly	perfectamente
personally	personalmente
possibly	posiblemente
previously	previamente
properly	adecuadamente
rarely	casi nunca
regularly	regularmente
seriously	en serio/seriamente
similarly	similar/del mismo modo
simply	simplemente
since	desde
slightly	levemente
specifically	específicamente
strongly	fuertemente
successfully	exitosamente
surely	seguramente
therefore	por lo tanto
this	este
though	sin embargo
throughout	a lo largo de
totally	totalmente
typically	típicamente

worldwide	mundial
worse	peor
worst	el peor
wrong	equivocado

B1 Adverbs Quiz

1.	aparte	A.	ahead
2.	cerca	B.	by
3.	efectivamente	C.	effectively
4.	adentro	D.	equally
5.	principalmente	E.	further
6.	por	F.	neither
7.	adecuadamente	G.	rarely
8.	casi nunca	H.	hardly
9.	más lejos	I.	this
10.	seguramente	J.	since
11.	equivocado	K.	totally
12.	sin embargo	L.	cheap
13.	equitativamente	M.	typically
14.	para siempre	N.	daily
15.	en la actualidad	O.	currently
16.	típicamente	P.	forever
17.	totalmente	Q.	surely
18.	este	R.	close
19.	dificilmente	S.	though
20.	desde	T.	wrong
21.	ni	U.	properly
22.	igualmente	V.	apart
23.	diario	W.	mainly
24.	barato	X.	indoors
25.	adelante	Y.	fairly

Answer Key

1. V
2. R
3. C
4. X
5. W
6. B
7. U
8. G
9. E
10. Q
11. T
12. S
13. Y
14. P
15. O
16. M
17. K
18. I
19. H
20. J
21. F
22. D
23. N
24. L
25. A

B1 Special Words

Pronouns

English Word	Spanish Translation
ours	nuestro
plenty	infinidad/mucho
theirs	suyo

Prepositions

English Word	Spanish Translation
despite	a pesar de
plus	más
throughout	a lo largo de
till	hasta
unlike	diferente a
upon	sobre
within	dentro de

Determiners

English Word	Spanish Translation
whatever	lo que sea

Conjunctions

English Word	Spanish Translation
nor	ni
now	ahora
once	una vez
except	excepto

Level B1 Vocabulary

though	sin embargo
till	hasta
unless	a no ser que/a menos que
whenever	cuando sea
whether	ya sea

B1 Vocabulary Final Exam

1. cadena	A. poverty
2. otorgar	B. highlight
3. tiempo libre	C. explode
4. prohibición	D. flood
5. localizar	E. share
6. pobreza	F. invest
7. explotar	G. flow
8. fluir	H. dislike
9. disgusto	I. murder
10. colgar	J. award
11. engañar	K. needle
12. disgustado	L. occur
13. medida	M. unlikely
14. improbable	N. unable
15. pálido	O. leisure
16. marco	P. tiny
17. valor	Q. hang
18. adelante	R. talented
19. espectador	S. ban
20. incapaz	T. violent
21. barato	U. ahead
22. picante	V. viewer
23. destacar	W. daily
24. igualmente	X. neither
25. ocurrir	Y. cheat
26. ni	Z. since
27. cuota	AA. frame
28. difícilmente	BB. this
29. tonto	CC. pale
30. inundación	DD. locate
31. talentoso	EE. totally
32. este	FF. tipically
33. tipicamente	GG. measure

34. aguja	HH. hardly
35. totalmente	II. equally
36. violento	JJ. spicy
37. desde	KK. cheap
38. invertir	LL. silly
39. diario	MM. update
40. diminuto	NN. worth
41. asesinato	OO. upset
42. actualizar	PP. string
43. enterrar	QQ. piel
44. clavo	RR. relate
45. en la actualidad	SS. sharp
46. para siempre	TT. rare
47. raro	UU. bury
48. fur	VV. forever
49. agudo	WW. currently
50. relatar	XX. pin

Answer Key

1.	PP		26.	X
2.	J		27.	E
3.	O		28.	HH
4.	S		29.	LL
5.	DD		30.	D
6.	A		31.	R
7.	C		32.	BB
8.	G		33.	FF
9.	H		34.	K
10.	Q		35.	EE
11.	Y		36.	T
12.	OO		37.	Z
13.	GG		38.	F
14.	M		39.	W
15.	CC		40.	P
16.	AA		41.	I
17.	NN		42.	MM
18.	U		43.	UU
19.	V		44.	XX
20.	N		45.	WW
21.	KK		46.	VV
22.	JJ		47.	TT
23.	B		48.	QQ
24.	II		49.	SS
25.	L		50.	RR

Level B2 Vocabulary

Spanish level B2 is the fourth level of Spanish in the CEFR. The official level description is "upper intermediate". At this level, students can function independently in a variety of settings, although with a limited success, especially in terms of precision. Once you obtain level B2, you can consider yourself as having gained basic fluency. Congratulations! You will, however, lack linguistic nuance and miss many subtle references. According to the official CEFR guidelines, someone at the B2 level in Spanish:

- Can understand the main ideas of complex text on both concrete and abstract topics, including technical discussions in his/her field of specialization (Council of Europe 2022).
- Can interact with a degree of fluency and spontaneity that makes regular interaction with native speakers quite possible without strain for either party (Council of Europe 2022).
- Can produce clear, detailed text on a wide range of subjects and explain a viewpoint on a topical issue giving the advantages and disadvantages of various options (Council of Europe 2022).

B2 Nouns

English Word	Spanish Translation
advance	avance/adelanto
affair	asunto
agency	agencia
agenda	agenda
aid	ayuda
aircraft	avión/aeronave
anger	enfado/cólera
angle	ángulo
anniversary	aniversario
appeal	apelación
approach	aproximación/enfoque
approval	aprobación
arms	brazos
aspect	aspecto
assessment	evaluación
association	asociación
attempt	intento/tentativa
attorney	abogado
bacteria	bacterias
barrier	barrera
beat	ritmo/latido
being	siendo
bet	apuesta
blame	culpa
bond	vínculo/enlace/bono
breast	seno/pecho
broadcast	emisión
budget	presupuesto
bullet	bala

bunch	racimo/manojo/grupo
burn	quemadura
bush	arbusto
cancer	cáncer
capacity	capacidad
capture	captura
cast	elenco
catch	captura
chairman	presidente
challenge	desafío
characteristic	característica
chief	jefe
chord	acorde
circumstance	circunstancia
citizen	ciudadano
classic	clásico
close	fin/final
collapse	colapso
combination	combinación
comfort	comodidad
command	dominio
commission	comisión
commitment	compromiso
committee	comité
complex	complejo
component	componente
concentration	concentración
concept	concepto
concern	preocupación
conduct	conducta
confidence	confianza
conflict	conflicto
congress	congreso

conservative	conservador
consideration	consideración
consonant	consonante
construction	construcción
contest	concurso
contract	contrato
contribution	contribución
core	núcleo
council	consejo
county	condado
courage	coraje/valor
crash	choque
crease	pliegue/arruga
creation	creación
creature	criatura
crew	tripulación
crisis	crisis
criterion	criterio
critic	crítica
criticism	crítica/criticism
crop	cultivo
cry	llorar
cure	cura/curación
current	actual
curve	curva
debate	debate
debt	deuda
decline	disminusión/descenso
decoration	decoración
decrease	disminución
defeat	derrota
defense	defensa
delay	demora
delivery	entrega

demand	demanda
depth	profundidad
desire	deseo
discipline	disciplina
disk	disco
display	visualización
distribution	distribución
divide	divisíon/brecha
division	división
dozen	docena
draft	borrador
ease	facilidad
edition	edición
emphasis	énfasis
encounter	encuentro
enthusiasm	entusiasmo
equal	igual
estate	bienes/inmuebles/finca
estimate	estimación
evil	mal
examination	examen
excuse	disculpa/escusa
executive	ejecutivo
exhibit	anexo
existence	existencia
expectation	expectativa
expense	gastos
exploration	exploración
extent	medida/extensión
extreme	extremo
facility	instalación/facilidad
failure	falla/fracaso
faith	fe

fault	culpa
feather	pluma
fee	tarifa
feed	alimentación
feedback	realimentación/feedback
feel	tacto/sensación
fig	higo
finance	finanzas
finding	hallazgo
firm	firme
flame	fuego
flash	destello
fold	doblez/pliegue
fortune	fortuna
freedom	libertad
frequency	frecuencia
fund	fondo
funding	fondos
gain	ganancia/aumento
gang	pandilla
genre	género
goods	bienes
governor	gobernador
grant	beca
guarantee	garantía
handle	mango/manija/asa
harm	daño
hearing	audiencia
heaven	cielo
heel	tacón
hell	infierno
high	máximo/elevado
hold	mantega
honor	honor

household	familiar/casa/familia
housing	alojamiento/viviendas
humor	humor
hunt	caza
hunting	caza
ideal	ideal
illustration	ilustración
imagination	imaginación
inch	pulgada
incident	incidente
income	ingreso
infection	infección
initiative	iniciativa
inquiry	consulta
insight	conocimiento
instance	instancia
institute	instituto
institution	institución
insurance	seguro
investigation	investigación
investment	inversión
joy	alegría
judgment	juicio
justice	justicia
labor	trabajo/mano de obra
landscape	paisaje
latest	el ultimo/más reciente
launch	lanzamiento
leadership	liderazgo
league	liga
leaves	hojas
license	licencia
load	carga

loan	préstamo
lord	señor
low	bajo
lung	pulmón
major	principal
majority	mayoria
make	marca
mass	masa
master	maestro
maximum	máximo
means	significa
measurement	medición
medium	medio
military	militar
mineral	mineral
minimum	mínimo
minister	ministro
minority	minoría
mission	misión
monitor	monitor
moral	moral
motion	movimiento
motor	motor
negative	negativo
nerve	nervio
nightmare	pesadilla
notion	noción
objective	objetivo
obligation	obligación
observation	observación
offense	ofensa
official	oficial
opening	apertura
opponent	adversario

opposition	oposición
organ	órgano
origin	origen
outcome	resultado
outline	contorno
oxygen	oxígeno
pace	paso
panel	panel
participant	partícipe
passage	paso
permit	permiso
perspective	perspectiva
phase	fase
phenomenon	fenómeno
philosophy	filosofía
pick	elección
pile	montón
pitch	tono/campo
plus	más
popularity	popularidad
positive	positivo
potential	potencial
praise	elogio/alabanza
preparation	preparación
presence	presencia
principle	principio
print	impresión
priority	prioridad
privacy	privacidad
procedure	procedimiento
professional	profesional
proof	prueba
proposal	propuesta

prospect	perspectiva
protection	proteccion
psychologist	psicólogo
psychology	psicología
publication	publicación
purchase	compra
rail	carril
rank	rango
reach	alcanze
reduction	reducción
regard	respecto
register	registro
regret	pesar/remordimiento
regulation	regulación
relief	alivio
remark	observación
representative	representante
reputation	reputación
requirement	requisito
rescue	rescate/salvamento
reserve	reserva
resident	residente
resort	complejo/recurso
revolution	revolución
reward	premio
rhythm	ritmo
rise	aumento/altura
root	raíz
round	ronda
rubber	caucho
rush	prisa
satellite	satélite
saving	ahorro
scale	escala

scream	chillido
sector	sector
selection	selección
self	sí mismo
senate	senado
senator	senador
sequence	secuencia
session	sesión
shade	sombra
shadow	sombra
shame	verguenza
shelter	abrigo
shock	conmoción
shooting	tiroteo
shore	orilla/costa
shot	disparo
silence	silencio
silk	seda
slide	deslizar
slope	pendiente
soul	alma
specialist	especialista
species	especies
split	división
sponsor	patrocinador
spread	untado
stand	posición/puesto
status	estado
steam	vapor
steel	acero
stock	valores
stream	arroyo
stretch	tramo

strike	huelga
struggle	lucha
sum	suma
surgery	cirugía
suspect	sospechar
switch	cambiar
syllable	sílaba
sympathy	compasión
tale	cuento
tank	tanque
tear	lágrima
therapy	terapia
threat	amenaza
tone	tono
transfer	transferencia/traslado
transition	transición
trial	juicio
trust	confianza
try	intento
tune	melodía
tunnel	túnel
universe	universo
van	camioneta
venue	evento
victory	victoria
violence	violencia
vision	visión
vitamin	vitamina
volume	volumen
wage	salario
weakness	debilidad
wealth	riqueza
whisper	susurro
wildlife	fauna silvestre

wire	cable/alambre
witness	testigo
worse	peor
worst	el peor
worth	valor
wound	herida
wrong	equivocado
zone	zona

B2 Nouns Quiz

1.	cable/alambre	A.	venue
2.	lágrima	B.	slope
3.	observación	C.	deslizar
4.	huelga	D.	stream
5.	respecto	E.	remark
6.	herida	F.	prospect
7.	elogio	G.	proposal
8.	untado	H.	strike
9.	movimiento	I.	outcome
10.	arroyo	J.	spread
11.	masa	K.	load
12.	salir	L.	insight
13.	mostrar	M.	steam
14.	evento	N.	display
15.	cultivo	O.	mass
16.	aprovación	P.	crop
17.	slide	Q.	wound
18.	ayuda	R.	approval
19.	intentar	S.	motion
20.	vapor	T.	attempt
21.	perspectiva	U.	wire
22.	conocimiento	V.	aid
23.	carga	W.	praise
24.	propuesta	X.	regard
25.	pendiente	Y.	tear

Answer Key

1. U
2. Y
3. E
4. H
5. X
6. Q
7. W
8. J
9. S
10. D
11. O
12. I
13. N
14. A
15. P
16. R
17. C
18. V
19. T
20. M
21. F
22. L
23. K
24. G
25. B

B2 Verbs

English Word	Spanish Translation
abandon	abandonar
accompany	acompañar
accuse	acusar
acknowledge	reconocer
acquire	adquirir
adapt	adaptar
adopt	adoptar
advance	avanzar
aid	ayudar
alarm	alarmar
alter	alterar
approach	acercarse
approve	aprobar
arise	surgir
assess	evaluar
associate	asociar
assume	asumir
attempt	intentar
bar	prohibir
battle	combatir
bear (deal with)	soportar
beg	rogar/mendigar
bet	apostar
blame	culpar
broadcast	transmitir
calculate	calcular
cancel	cancelar
capture	capturar
cast	lanzar

chair	presidir
challenge	desafiar
cite	citar
collapse	colapsar/derrumbarse
comfort	confortar
command	comandar/ordenar/mandar
conduct	conducir
construct	construir
contest	Impugner/disputar/concursar
contract	contratar
contribute	contribuir
convert	convertir
crash	chocar
credit	acreditar
criticize	criticar
cure	curar
curve	curvar
date	fechar/salir con
debate	debater
declare	declarar
decline	rechazar
decorate	decorar
decrease	disminuir
defeat	vencer
defend	defender
delay	retrasar/demorar
demand	demander/pedir/exigir
demonstrate	demostrar
deny	negar
desert	abandonar
deserve	merecer
desire	desear
detail	detallar

detect	detectar
differ	ser distinto/diferir de
dig	excavar
discount	descontar
dismiss	descartar
display	mostrar
distribute	distribuir
document	documentar
dominate	dominar
drag	arrastrar
ease	aliviar
edit	editar
elect	elegir
emerge	surgir
emphasize	enfatizar
enable	habilitar
encounter	encontrar
engage	comprometer
enhance	mejorar
ensure	asegurar
equate	equiparar
establish	establecer
estimate	estimar
evaluate	evaluar
excuse	disculpar
exhibit	exhibir
exit	salir
expose	exponer
extend	extender
favor	favorecer
figure	figurar
file	archivar
finance	financiar
flash	parpadear

float	flotar
forgive	perdonar
found	encontrado
free	liberar
function	funcionar
fund	financiar
gain	ganar
generate	generar
govern	gobernar
grab	agarrar
grade	calificar
grant	otorgar
guarantee	garantizar
handle	encargarse de
harm	herir
heard	oído
hesitate	dudar
honor	honrar
host	hospedar
illustrate	ilustrar
imply	implicar
impose	imponer
impress	impresionar
inform	informar
insist	insistir
inspire	inspirar
install	instalar
interpret	interpretar
interrupt	interrumpir
issue	emitir/expedir
justify	justificar
launch	lanzar
lean	inclinarse

level	nivelar
line	alinear
load	cargar
lower	reducer/bajar/disminuir
maintain	mantener
master	dominar
melt	fundir
model	modelar
modify	modificar
monitor	monitor
mount	montar
multiply	multiplicar
narrow	estrechar
obey	obedecer
object	oponerse a
observe	observar
obtain	obtener
offend	ofender
operate	funcionar/operar
oppose	oponerse a
owe	deber
package	empacar
permit	permitir
picture	fotografiar
pile	apilar
populate	poblar
pose	posar/plantear
position	posicionar
possess	poseer
power	prender
praise	elogiar
preserve	preservar
process	proyectar
project	proyecto

propose	proponer
purchase	comprar
pursue	perseguir
range	variar/oscilar
rank	clasificar
rate	calificar
recall	recordar
recover	recuperar
regard	considerar
register	registrarse
regret	arrepentirse
rely	confiar
remark	observar
rescue	rescatar
reserve	reservar
resist	resistir
resolve	resolver
retain	retener
reveal	revelar
reward	recompensar
rid	librar
rub	frotar
rush	apurarse
sample	probar/muestrear
satisfy	satisfacer
schedule	programar
scream	gritar
seat	sentarse
secure	asegurar
seek	buscar
select	seleccionar
sense	sentir
sentence	sentenciar

settle	resolver
shape	dar forma
shift	cambiar
ship	enviar
shock	impactar
slide	deslizar
slip	resbalar
slope	inclinarse
speed	acelerar
split	separar
sponsor	patrocinar
spot	detectar/manchar
stage	organizar
stare	mirar fijamente
stretch	estirar
strike	golpear/atacar
structure	estructurar
struggle	luchar
stuff	rellenar
submit	enviar
sum	resumir
surround	rodear
survey	encuestar
suspect	sospechar
swear	jurar
sweep	barrer
target	apuntar
tear	rasgar
threaten	amenazar
title	titular
transfer	transferir
transform	transformar
trouble	complicar
trust	confiar

urge	urgir
value	valorar
vary	variar
whisper	susurrar
wind	enrollar
witness	presenciar/testificar
Wound	herir
wrap	envolver

B2 Verbs Quiz

1.	acusar	A.	cast
2.	mendigar	B.	imply
3.	calcular	C.	pursue
4.	emitir	D.	calculate
5.	rechazar	E.	recover
6.	negar	F.	rely
7.	excavar	G.	retain
8.	habilitar	H.	gain
9.	ganar	I.	settle
10.	dudar	J.	accuse
11.	implicar	K.	slip
12.	obedecer	L.	trust
13.	buscar	M.	enable
14.	recuperar	N.	transfer
15.	confiar	O.	beg
16.	retener	P.	generate
17.	sentarse	Q.	sweep
18.	resolver	R.	assume
19.	enviar	S.	decline
20.	resbalar	T.	ship
21.	barrer	U.	hesitate
22.	confianza	V.	seat
23.	transferir	W.	deny
24.	generar	X.	obey
25.	asumir	Y.	dig

Answer Key

1. J
2. O
3. D
4. A
5. S
6. W
7. Y
8. M
9. H
10. U
11. B
12. X
13. C
14. E
15. F
16. G
17. V
18. I
19. T
20. K
21. Q
22. L
23. N
24. P
25. R

B2 Adjectives

English Word	Spanish Translation
absolute	absoluto
acceptable	aceptable
accurate	preciso
actual	actual
additional	adicional
advance	ventaja
aggressive	agresivo
annual	anual
anxious	ansioso
apparent	aparente
appropriate	adecuado
armed	armado
artificial	artificial
artistic	artístico
ashamed	avergonzado
associated	asociado
bent	doblado
bitter	amargo
blind	ciego
brief	breve
broad	amplio
capable	capaz
characteristic	característica
chief	jefe
civil	civil
classic	clásico
complicated	complicado
concerned	preocupado
confusing	confuso

conscious	consciente
conservative	conservador
consistent	coherente
constant	constante
contemporary	contemporáneo
convinced	convencido
core	núcleo
corporate	corporativo
critical	crítico
crucial	crucial
curved	curvo
decent	decente
decimal	decimal
deliberate	deliberado
depressed	deprimido
depressing	deprimente
desperate	desesperado
detailed	detallado
dishonest	deshonesto
domestic	doméstico
downward	hacia abajo
dramatic	dramático
efficient	eficiente
elderly	anciano
emotional	emocional
enthusiastic	entusiasta
entire	completo
ethical	ético
even	incluso
evil	mal
executive	ejecutivo
external	externo
extraordinary	extraordinario

flexible	flexible
folding	plegable
former	anterior
forward	hacia adelante
fundamental	fundamental
grand	grandioso/gran
harmful	dañino
hollow	hueco
holy	santo
humorous	humorístico
impatient	impaciente
impressed	impresionado
industrial	industrial
initial	inicial
inner	interno
intended	destinado
intense	intenso
internal	interno
junior	júnior
limited	limitado
lively	dinámico/animado
logical	lógico
lone	solitario
long-term	a largo plazo
loose	suelto/flojo
mass	masa
massive	masivo
material	material
maximum	máximo
military	militar
minimum	mínimo
minor	menor
mixed	mezclado
moral	moral

multiple	múltiple
mysterious	misterioso
national	nacional
numerous	numeroso
objective	objetivo
offensive	ofensivo
opposed	opuesto
outer	exterior
overall	general
patient	paciente
permanent	permanente
plain	plano/simple
plus	más
pointed	puntiagudo
potential	potencial
pregnant	embarazada
prime	principal
principal	principal
pure	puro
rapid	rápido
raw	crudo
realistic	realista
reasonable	razonable
regional	regional
relevant	importante
representative	representante
resident	residente
routine	rutina
rubber	de goma
rural	rural
satisfied	satisfecho
secure	seguro
senior	sénior

sensitive	sensitivo
severe	severo
shallow	poco profundo
shocked	conmocionado
significant	significativo/importante
sincere	sincero
slight	leve/ligero
solar	solar
specialist	especialista
spiritual	espiritual
stable	estable
steady	firme
steep	empinado/escarpado
sticky	pegajoso
stiff	rígido
strict	estricto
surrounding	circundante
temporary	temporario
tough	difícil/duro/resistente
tropical	tropical
unconscious	inconsciente
unexpected	inesperado
unique	único
unknown	desconocido
upper	superior
urban	urbano
vast	enorme
very	muy
virtual	virtual
visual	visual
vital	vital
wealthy	rico
willing	dispuesto
wise	sabio

B2 Adjectives Quiz

1.	superior	A.	vast
2.	estricto	B.	steady
3.	exterior	C.	shallow
4.	crudo	D.	inner
5.	interno	E.	outer
6.	sabio	F.	holy
7.	deprimido	G.	upper
8.	principal	H.	elderly
9.	preocupado	I.	complicated
10.	firme	J.	raw
11.	amargo	K.	classic
12.	complicado	L.	wise
13.	enorme	M.	bent
14.	ansioso	N.	depressed
15.	importante	O.	prime
16.	armado	P.	accurate
17.	solitario	Q.	unique
18.	preciso	R.	armed
19.	dispuesto	S.	lone
20.	doblado	T.	anxious
21.	clásico	U.	strict
22.	poco profundo	V.	bitter
23.	anciano	W.	willing
24.	único	X.	concerned
25.	santo	Y.	relevant

Answer Key

1. G
2. U
3. E
4. J
5. D
6. L
7. N
8. O
9. X
10. B
11. V
12. I
13. A
14. T
15. Y
16. R
17. S
18. P
19. W
20. M
21. K
22. C
23. H
24. Q
25. F

B2 Adverbs

English Word	Spanish Translation
abroad	en el extranjero
afterward	después
apparently	aparentemente
aside	aparte
basically	básicamente
beyond	más allá de
closely	cercanamente
commonly	comúnmente
constantly	constantemente
deeply	profundamente
deliberately	deliberadamente
downward	hacia abajo
elsewhere	en otra parte
entirely	enteramente
fully	completamente
furthermore	además
gradually	gradualmente
increasingly	cada vez más
initially	inicialmente
largely	en gran parte
long-term	a largo plazo
nevertheless	a pesar de eso
occasionally	ocasionalmente
otherwise	de lo contrario
overall	general/total
partly	parcialmente
rapidly	rápidamente
relatively	relativamente

significantly	significativamente
somewhat	algo
thus	por lo tanto
truly	verdaderamente
ultimately	por último
upward	hacia arriba
way	forma
widely	ampliamente

B2 Adverbs Quiz

1.	más allá de	A.	abroad
2.	a largo plazo	B.	fully
3.	general	C.	way
4.	forma	D.	closely
5.	después	E.	nevertheless
6.	en el extranjero	F.	long-term
7.	en otra parte	G.	somewhat
8.	algo	H.	rapidly
9.	a pesar de eso	I.	beyond
10.	profundamente	J.	initially
11.	hacia arriba	K.	overall
12.	relativamente	L.	downward
13.	aparte	M.	thus
14.	además	N.	partly
15.	hacia abajo	O.	deliberately
16.	gradualmente	P.	aside
17.	parcialmente	Q.	furthermore
18.	completamente	R.	relatively
19.	deliberadamente	S.	widely
20.	inicialmente	T.	upward
21.	rápidamente	U.	deeply
22.	de lo contrario	V.	elsewhere
23.	cercanamente	W.	afterward
24.	ampliamente	X.	gradually
25.	por lo tanto	Y.	otherwise

Answer Key

1. I
2. F
3. K
4. C
5. W
6. A
7. V
8. G
9. E
10. U
11. T
12. R
13. P
14. Q
15. L
16. X
17. N
18. B
19. O
20. J
21. H
22. Y
23. D
24. S
25. M

B2 Special Words

Pronouns

English Word	Spanish Translation
whom	a quién

Prepositions

English Word	Spanish Translation
beyond	más allá de
but	pero
following	siguiente
via	a través de

Conjunctions

English Word	Spanish Translation
plus	más
though	aunque
whereas	mientras que
wherever	donde quiera
yet	todavía

B2 Vocabulary Final Exam

1. cultivo	A. approval
2. superior	B. strict
3. mendigar	C. enable
4. exterior	D. outer
5. estricto	E. inner
6. ayuda	F. aid
7. además	G. downward
8. calcular	H. gradually
9. sabio	I. calculate
10. propuesta	J. partly
11.principal	K. furthermore
12. hacia abajo	L. venue
13. intentar	M. deppresed
14. gradualmente	N. beg
15. emitir	O. upper
16. completamente	P. proposal
17. pendiente	Q. bitter
18. deprimido	R. imply
19. parcialmente	S. crop
20. evento	T. fully
21. deliberadamente	U. cast
22. ganar	V. closely
23. de lo contrario	W. load
24. aprovación	X. widely
25. amargo	Y. decline
26. habilitar	Z. thus
27. firme	AA. attempt/try
28. carga	BB. way
29. cercanamente	CC. otherwise
30. interno	DD. accuse
31. negar	EE. initially
32. por lo tanto	FF. deliberately
33. deslizar	GG. slope

34. forma	HH. steady
35. excavar	II. gain
36. ampliamente	JJ. deny
37. rechazar	KK. concerned
38. inicialmente	LL. prime
39. preocupado	MM. slide
40. vapor	NN. raw
41. crudo	OO. dig
42. acusar	PP. steam
43. perspectiva	QQ. doubt
44. complicado	RR. imply
45. dudar	SS. vast
46. rapidamente	TT. rapidly
47. obedecer	UU. obey
48. conocimiento	VV. complicated
49.enorme	WW. perspective
50. implicar	XX. knowledge

Answer Key

1.	S		26.	C
2.	O		27.	HH
3.	N		28.	W
4.	D		29.	V
5.	B		30.	E
6.	F		31.	JJ
7.	K		32.	Z
8.	I		33.	MM
9.	R		34.	BB
10.	P		35.	OO
11.	LL		36.	X
12.	G		37.	Y
13.	AA		38.	EE
14.	H		39.	KK
15.	U		40.	PP
16.	T		41.	NN
17.	GG		42.	DD
18.	M		43.	WW
19.	J		44.	VV
20.	L		45.	QQ
21.	FF		46.	TT
22.	II		47.	UU
23.	CC		48.	XX
24.	A		49.	SS
25.	Q		50.	R

Cumulative Final Exam

1.	fabricar/hacer		A.	know
2.	necesidad		B.	make
3.	carne de res		C.	give
4.	desierto		D.	join
5.	saber		E.	beef
6.	explicación		F.	bone
7.	dar		G.	go
8.	brecha		H.	average
9.	unirse		I.	explanation
10.	lata		J.	need
11.	promedio		K.	gap
12.	ventaja		L.	can
13.	ir		M.	fork
14.	manera		N.	visit
15.	comportamiento		O.	advantage
16.	por ciento		P.	see
17.	salto		Q.	percent
18.	visitar		R.	behavior
19.	esperanza		S.	have
20.	tenedor		T.	jump
21.	hueso		U.	manner
22.	tener		V.	drive
23.	ver		W.	hope
24.	poner		X.	desert
25.	conducir		Y.	put

26.	tienda	A.	store
27.	fiesta	B.	year
28.	tio	C.	rice
29.	cocina	D.	kitchen
30.	chica/muchacha	E.	drink
31.	vuelo	F.	girl
32.	casa	G.	bill
33.	contar	H.	classroom
34.	hervir	I.	greet
35.	saludar	J.	lift
36.	tirar	K.	rise
37.	tocar	L.	advertise
38.	gestionar	M.	manage
39.	aeropuerto	N.	touch
40.	anunciar	O.	reply
41.	responder	P.	pull
42.	aumentar	Q.	boil
43.	levantar/elevar	R.	count
44.	salon de clases	S.	house
45.	factura	T.	flight
46.	risa	U.	airport
47.	bebida	V.	laughter
48.	arroz	W.	uncle
49.	año	X.	party
50.	pollo	Y.	chicken

51.	lana	A.	needle
52.	aguja	B.	sample
53.	impuesto	C.	highlight
54.	destacar	D.	script
55.	superficie	E.	accuse
56.	acusar	F.	shift
57.	cambio	G.	cast
58.	mendigar	H.	surface
59.	texto	I.	deny
60.	calcular	J.	tax
61.	muestra	K.	dig
62.	emitir	L.	wool
63.	fila	M.	enable
64.	rechazar	N.	youth
65.	liberación	O.	gain
66.	dudar	P.	plot
67.	implicar	Q.	imply
68.	cita	R.	hesitate
69.	ganar	S.	press
70.	juventud	T.	decline
71.	habilitar	U.	quote
72.	prensa	V.	calculate
73.	excavar	W.	release
74.	negar	X.	beg
75.	trama	Y.	row

76.	colgar	A.	roll
77.	observación	B.	wire
78.	relatar	C.	convince
79.	huelga	D.	remark
80.	convencer	E.	relate
81.	respecto	F.	regard
82.	rodar	G.	hang
83.	untado	H.	wound
84.	advertir	I.	warn
85.	movimiento	J.	praise
86.	preguntarse	K.	wonder
87.	masa	L.	stream
88.	intercambiar	M.	contact
89.	cultivo	N.	crop
90.	donar	O.	separate
91.	arroyo	P.	mass
92.	veneno	Q.	claim
93.	elogio	R.	motion
94.	sujetar	S.	fasten
95.	herida	T.	spread
96.	contacto	U.	poison
97.	lágrima	V.	strike
98.	separar	W.	donate
99.	cable/alambre	X.	tear
100.	reclamar	Y.	trade

101.	implicar	A.	obey
102.	transferir	B.	transfer
103.	obedecer	C.	recover
104.	generar	D.	assume
105.	buscar	E.	rely
106.	asumir	F.	fur
107.	recuperar	G.	retain
108.	piel	H.	pin
109.	confiar	I.	viewer
110.	medida	J.	settle
111.	retener	K.	frame
112.	tiempo libre	L.	dislike
113.	sentarse	M.	trust
114.	cadena	N.	poverty
115.	resolver	O.	update
116.	actualizar	P.	sweep
117.	confianza	Q.	string
118.	pobreza	R.	leisure
119.	enviar	S.	slip
120.	disgusto	T.	measure
121.	marco	U.	generate
122.	resbalar	V.	ship
123.	espectador	W.	seat
124.	clavo	X.	pursue
125.	barrer	Y.	imply

126.	oscuro	A.	bored
127.	costoso	B.	dark
128.	amistoso	C.	tired
129.	seguro	D.	useful
130.	tarde	E.	friendly
131.	repentinamente	F.	expensive
132.	limpio	G.	clean
133.	pasado	H.	sure
134.	casado	I.	poor
135.	bajo	J.	somewhere
136.	pobre	K.	suddenly
137.	menos	L.	hungry
138.	hambriento	M.	loud
139.	pequeño	N.	quiet
140.	tranquilo	O.	last
141.	último	P.	angry
142.	enojado	Q.	little
143.	fuerte	R.	rich
144.	rico	S.	less
145.	exterior	T.	interesting
146.	interesante	U.	low
147.	algún lado	V.	overseas
148.	cansado	W.	married
149.	útil	X.	past
150.	aburrido	Y.	late

151.	raro	A.	neat
152.	inteligente	B.	basic
153.	gradualmente	C.	glad
154.	pálido	D.	mild
155.	parcialmente	E.	sudden
156.	ordenado	F.	engaged
157.	completamente	G.	clever
158.	nivel	H.	gradually
159.	inicialmente	I.	pale
160.	leve	J.	partly
161.	contento	K.	otherwise
162.	rápidamente	L.	rare
163.	comprometido	M.	closely
164.	de lo contrario	N.	thus
165.	ampliamente	O.	level
166.	molesto	P.	widely
167.	bruto	Q.	rapidly
168.	por lo tanto	R.	annoying
169.	asombrado	S.	initially
170.	repentino	T.	deliberately
171.	cercanamente	U.	folk
172.	gente	V.	fully
173.	deliberadamente	W.	rough
174.	orgulloso	X.	proud
175.	básico	Y.	amazed

176.	firme	A.	upper
177.	amargo	B.	complicated
178.	superior	C.	raw
179.	ansioso	D.	prospect
180.	importante	E.	insight
181.	estricto	F.	inner
182.	perspectiva	G.	load
183.	carga	H.	proposal
184.	exterior	I.	wise
185.	pendiente	J.	slope
186.	prohibición	K.	bitter
187.	crudo	L.	depressed
188.	enterrar	M.	explode
189.	invertir	N.	bury
190.	interno	O.	prime
191.	inundación	P.	invest
192.	explotar	Q.	relevant
193.	sabio	R.	concerned
194.	propuesta	S.	flood
195.	conocimiento	T.	steady
196.	deprimido	U.	ban
197.	enorme	V.	outer
198.	complicado	W.	anxious
199.	principal	X.	vast
200.	preocupado	Y.	strict

201.	sujetar	A.	claim
202.	realmente	B.	decline
203.	emitir	C.	anymore
204.	contacto	D.	separate
205.	ya no	E.	recently
206.	seguramente	F.	job
207.	separar	G.	week
208.	visitar	H.	contact
209.	nombre	I.	avoid
210.	reclamar	J.	contain
211.	empujar	K.	fasten
212.	aparecer	L.	appear
213.	votar	M.	push
214.	contener	N.	vote
215.	evitar	O.	predict
216.	acusar	P.	name
217.	predecir	Q.	beg
218.	semana	R.	map
219.	trabajo	S.	visit
220.	mendigar	T.	calculate
221.	mapa	U.	either
222.	hace poco	V.	certainly
223.	cualquiera	W.	accuse
224.	calcular	X.	actually
225.	rechazar	Y.	cast

226.	arroyo	A.	display
227.	en otra parte	B.	abroad
228.	relatar	C.	convince
229.	convencer	D.	outcome
230.	masa	E.	roll
231.	preguntarse	F.	trade
232.	disgusto	G.	dislike
233.	salir	H.	mass
234.	repentinamente	I.	poverty
235.	pasado	J.	update
236.	gratis	K.	string
237.	mostrar	L.	wonder
238.	seguro	M.	stream
239.	cadena	N.	free
240.	evento	O.	pass
241.	advertir	P.	suddenly
242.	actualizar	Q.	sure
243.	resbalar	R.	venue
244.	tiempo libre	S.	leisure
245.	pobreza	T.	warn
246.	intercambiar	U.	relate
247.	generar	V.	slip
248.	rodar	W.	somewhat
249.	algo	X.	elsewhere
250.	en el extranjero	Y.	generate

Answer Key

1. B	34. Q	67. Q
2. J	35. I	68. U
3. E	36. P	69. O
4. X	37. N	70. N
5. A	38. M	71. M
6. I	39. U	72. S
7. C	40. L	73. K
8. K	41. O	74. I
9. D	42. K	75. P
10. L	43. J	76. G
11. H	44. H	77. D
12. O	45. G	78. E
13. G	46. V	79. V
14. U	47. E	80. C
15. R	48. C	81. F
16. Q	49. B	82. A
17. T	50. Y	83. T
18. N	51. L	84. I
19. W	52. A	85. R
20. M	53. J	86. K
21. F	54. C	87. P
22. S	55. H	88. Y
23. P	56. E	89. N
24. Y	57. F	90. W
25. V	58. X	91. L
26. A	59. D	92. U
27. X	60. V	93. J
28. W	61. B	94. S
29. D	62. G	95. H
30. F	63. Y	96. M
31. T	64. T	97. X
32. S	65. W	98. O
33. R	66. R	99. B

100.	Q	136.	I	172.	U
101.	Y	137.	S	173.	T
102.	B	138.	L	174.	X
103.	A	139.	Q	175.	B
104.	U	140.	N	176.	T
105.	X	141.	O	177.	K
106.	D	142.	P	178.	A
107.	C	143.	M	179.	W
108.	F	144.	R	180.	Q
109.	E	145.	V	181.	Y
110.	T	146.	T	182.	D
111.	G	147.	J	183.	G
112.	R	148.	C	184.	V
113.	W	149.	D	185.	J
114.	Q	150.	A	186.	U
115.	J	151.	L	187.	C
116.	O	152.	G	188.	N
117.	M	153.	H	189.	P
118.	N	154.	I	190.	F
119.	V	155.	J	191.	S
120.	L	156.	A	192.	M
121.	K	157.	V	193.	I
122.	S	158.	O	194.	H
123.	I	159.	S	195.	E
124.	H	160.	D	196.	L
125.	P	161.	C	197.	X
126.	B	162.	Q	198.	B
127.	F	163.	F	199.	O
128.	E	164.	K	200.	R
129.	H	165.	P	201.	K
130.	Y	166.	R	202.	X
131.	K	167.	W	203.	Y
132.	G	168.	N	204.	H
133.	X	169.	Y	205.	C
134.	W	170.	E	206.	V
135.	U	171.	M	207.	D

208.	S	223.	U	238.	Q
209.	P	224.	T	239.	K
210.	A	225.	B	240.	R
211.	M	226.	M	241.	T
212.	L	227.	X	242.	J
213.	N	228.	U	243.	V
214.	J	229.	C	244.	S
215.	I	230.	H	245.	I
216.	W	231.	L	246.	F
217.	O	232.	G	247.	Y
218.	G	233.	D	248.	E
219.	F	234.	P	249.	W
220.	Q	235.	O	250.	B
221.	R	236.	N		
222.	E	237.	A		

Conclusion

So, there you have it. I hope this book met your expectations and you learned a great deal of vocabulary. I believe I wrote a useful book and am certain that if you spend between one and three months consistently studying, you will have earned a level of Spanish vocabulary enabling you to understand the most commonly used words. That does not mean you will be fluent in Spanish, but you will have an exceptionally strong foundational vocabulary.

I have developed a basic website you can visit at www.nothingbutvocab.com. You may sign up to receive emails to learn about my upcoming new books. There is also a resource tab with a list of movies, podcasts, YouTube channels, and TV shows I recommend. It is critical that you practice what you have learned, or you will not only cease advancing, you will lose what you have worked so hard to gain.

I intend to continually improve and expand this book in future editions. As such, if you find an error, have suggestions, or good ideas for future editions, please send me an email. I will try to incorporate all suggestions, criticisms, and fix the errors you point out in the next edition. You may reach me at John@NothingbutVocab.com. Furthermore, if you have a moment to spare, I would genuinely appreciate an honest book review. Just a few words would suffice.

Thanks again for reading!

Printed in Great Britain
by Amazon